GHOST STORIES

and Mysterious Creatures of

BRITISH COLUMBIA

BARBARA SMITH

First printed in 1999 10 9 8 7 6 5 4 3 2

Printed in Canada

The Publisher: Lone Pine Publishing

10145 - 81 Avenue
Edmonton, AB T6E 1W9
Canada

#202A, 1110 Seymour St.
Vancouver, BC V6B 3N3
Canada

1901 Raymond Ave. SW, Suite C
Renton, WA 98055
USA

Lone Pine Publishing website: http://www.lonepinepublishing.com

Canadian Cataloguing in Publication Data

Smith, Barbara, 1947-
Ghost stories and mysterious creatures of British Columbia

ISBN 1-55105-172-9

1. Legends—British Columbia. 2. Ghosts—British Columbia. I. Title.
GR580.S64 1999 398.2'0971105 C99-910888-3

Editorial Director: Nancy Foulds
Production Manager: Jody Reekie
Editorial: Volker Bodegom
Layout & Production: Volker Bodegom, Michelle Bynoe
Photo Credits: Robert Smith, except: B.C. Archives (pp. 45, 50, 90, 145); B.C. Heritage (pp. 57, 103); Quesnel and District Museum (pp. 53, 67); George Rieder/Guisachan House (p. 143); Dolores Steele (pp. 156, 176); Volker Bodegom (pp. 202, 209, 231).

The publisher acknowledges the financial support of the Government of Canada through the Book Publishing Industry Development Program (BPIDP) for its publishing activities.

PC: P6

Canada

Dedication

This book is dedicated to the memory of Sylvia and Henry Trumbley.

For my grandsons and their peers—who will need forests as much as books—arrangements have been made to plant trees to compensate for those used in publishing this volume.

Contents

Acknowledgements

I wish to thank the following people for their assistance in compiling this volume: the staff at the Fernie Chamber of Commerce; John Kinnear of Fernie; my friend, Dr. Barrie Robinson of Edmonton; and, as always, that skilful and tenacious paranormal researcher, W. Ritchie Benedict of Calgary. Ritchie, your abilities are exceeded only by your generosity. Thank you.

Finally, my efforts would be pointless without the continuing support from all the talented people at Lone Pine Publishing, whose labours on my behalf are extraordinary and deeply appreciated. Thank you, one and all.

Introduction

Compiling and writing a book about paranormal happenings in "Super Natural British Columbia" was a most intriguing and appealing prospect. Reality more than lived up to my anticipation. The project was both engrossing and entertaining to work on but, now that I've finished researching and writing the book, I am somewhat surprised to find that I have more questions about the extraordinary than I started with. Even though this is my sixth book of true paranormal stories (after *Ghost Stories of Alberta*, *More Ghost Stories of Alberta*, *Ghost Stories of Manitoba*, *Ontario Ghost Stories* and *Ghost Stories of the Rocky Mountains*), as I did the research, a part of me was still naïvely hoping to find explanations for paranormal phenomenon. No such luck. If, to quote the popular television show, *The X-Files*, "the truth is out there," I have yet to find it.

My interest in the paranormal and local folklore is propelled by a combined passion for history and mystery. Elusive answers did not dampen the fun of the search nor limit the enormous range of stories that I unearthed. Those tales that are included are, I feel, representative—geographically, historically and by type of phenomenon—of those that relate to this western province.

Since the bulk of the stories in this book are ghost stories, ideally we should begin by arriving at a satisfactory definition of the term "ghost." Over the past ten years, I've devoted much effort to searching out that definition. Unfortunately, I'm not sure that I'm much closer to finding it now than when I started. This lack of certainty also extends to several connected questions: Why are ghosts here? Why are some people so much more likely than others to see a ghost? Why are some places haunted, though others may have seen more traumatic events and yet remain 'cold' (i.e., not haunted)?

I have, however, developed some firm theories as to what a ghost is not. A ghost is not a cute, white cartoon character, nor is it a human figure draped in a white sheet. A ghost is also not necessarily a filmy, gauzy apparition, although certainly some fit that description.

Frederic Myers, one of the founding members of the old and honourable Society for Psychical Research in England, suggested in his book *Human Personality and Its Survival of Bodily Death* (1903) that a ghost is "an indication that some kind of force is being exercised after death" and that this force "is in some way connected with a person" now deceased. He further purported that ghosts are unaware of themselves and incapable of thought.

With all due respect to the erudite Dr. Myers, I wonder whether that last statement is one hundred percent true in all cases of hauntings. Some ghosts seem only to be continuing on with their life's business, completely oblivious to the world of the living that surrounds them, but others have specific tasks that they are determined to perform, such as delivering a message.

An issue of semantics arises in retelling ghost stories. There are few true synonyms in the English language, but I have chosen to use the following words interchangeably: spectre, spirit, entity, presence, manifestation, phantom, spirit, wraith and ghost.

Not all ghosts present themselves visually in the shape of humans. Those that do are more properly called apparitions. Just because a ghost is not seen does not mean one is not present. The spectre may manifest only in the form of a sensation—that feeling that one is not alone despite the fact that no one else is physically present. Ghosts can also manifest as odours—both pleasant and unpleasant. Other evidence of a paranormal occurrence can include ghostly lights and phantom music.

A poltergeist is a rare type of spectral being that can be identified by its noisy and possibly violent behaviours. It will often move objects and can actually wreak havoc on its surrounding environment. Poltergeists are associated with people rather than places. They have been known to follow people for years, even through a succession of moves from one residence to another.

Retrocognition, which has been described as seeing or in some other manner sensing the past, is an especially fascinating type of ghostly encounter. Some students of the paranormal believe that most, if not all, hauntings are a result of retrocognition. The phenomenon is thought to be the result of a person's temporary displacement in time that allows the person affected an opportunity to review or experience historical events.

There are some famous and well-documented cases of retrocognition. One, which took place in the summer of 1901, involves Eleanor Jourdain and Annie Moberly, two professors from England who were visiting Versailles, France. As the women strolled throughout the gardens in the vicinity of the Petit and Grand Trianons, they became suddenly and inexplicably disoriented.

They saw their surroundings in a strange, dreamlike fashion and observed, in a detached way, people dressed in a style from two centuries before their era, milling about a kiosk and a small bridgelike structure. As quickly and as spontaneously as their shared hallucination began, it ceased. They saw that they were still in the same gardens as in that earlier time, but the "bridge" and kiosk were no longer there and those wandering about wore contemporary clothing.

Intrigued by what had just happened to them, Jourdain and Moberly revisited the site and experienced retrocognition again.

Upon their return home, they reported their visions to colleagues. As word spread, others, interested in the professors' strange descriptions, travelled to the site, where they too saw, and even spoke to, people from an era long past.

An equally famous example of this supernatural phenomenon also occurred in France, on August 19, 1951. Two women, who've become known as the Norton sisters, were visiting Dieppe. They were sleeping in their hotel room when, without warning, they heard an air raid taking place nearby. The sounds of shellfire, dive-bombing and people screaming were unmistakable and continued for three hours in the very early morning. The sisters were experiencing auditory retrocognition, for the attack that they were listening to had actually taken place in 1942.

It has been suggested that retrocognition (also known as postcognition) actually occurs much more frequently than is commonly recognized, but the fleeting temporal displacement is simply written off to the witness's imagination. If that is so, perhaps we should be paying closer attention to momentary shifts in our perception when we experience them.

The opposite of retrocognition is precognition—seeing or sensing an event that has not yet occurred. When such an experience is accompanied by a presence, that presence is called a forerunner.

One further manifestation of phantom energy is the existence of ghost lights or ignes fatui. These luminous paranormal occurrences have entranced people over the centuries. Some of the stories in this book include references to this phenomena; the tale about the ill-fated and very haunted Beckley Farm is one of the best examples of this paranormal oddity.

But why do any of this ghostly phenomena exist? "Leftover energy" (physical and emotional) is a theory used to explain the existence of ghosts. This theory is closely related to the "psychic imprint" proposition—that the essence of a person or an event has somehow been "stamped" onto the environment in which that person lived or the event occurred. The deceased person's soul has effectively left an imprint on the physical world. He or she has become a ghost. Traumatic or violent events can also leave such a mark, resulting in a place being haunted.

According to some students of the subject, ghosts are beings who either don't know that the body that they once occupied is deceased, or who can't accept death because they feel obligated to complete unfinished business among the living.

Another theory holds that ghosts are disembodied souls (or energies, personalities or spirits) that are usually detectable only by our (nearly atrophied) sixth sense. Rather than perceiving this other-worldly sensation with our usual and familiar five senses, we may only notice the hair on our arms or on the back of our necks standing on end or be aware of a tingling sensation in our skin. Or we might experience that decidedly disconcerting feeling that we are not alone or that we are being watched, even though our other senses fail to confirm the existence of any other presence near us. Scientists have suggested that humans do possess a rarely used sixth sense located in the vomeronasal organ (in the nose) that is capable of detecting pheromones—chemicals released into the air in minute quantities by many species as a way of communicating with others of their kind.

Perhaps the vomeronasal organ also detects or senses energies exuded from disembodied spirits but, since we are unused to consciously responding to messages from this sense, we are often unable to recognize the messages, aside from being aware that "something" is close to us. Children seem to be more sensitive to other-worldly presences than are adults. Perhaps it is because children are more sensitive to messages received from their vomeronasal organs. Over time, adults come to rely more on their other five senses and to ignore or fail to respond as much to sensations picked up by their sixth sense. Those adults who do seem to recognize and rely upon messages from their sixth sense are often referred to as "sensitives." Though this sensitivity seems to be inborn, it can apparently be enhanced with practice (or diminished through neglect). Perhaps the variation in sensitivity from person to person explains why some people are more likely than others to encounter a ghost.

Throughout all of these suppositions lurks a further mystery: Does a ghostly encounter originate with the living person who is experiencing the encounter, or with the ghost itself? Perhaps that point is debatable but, because many people report seeing or sensing the same spirit either at the same or different times, the entity is unlikely to be merely a figment of the observer's imagination.

Being haunted is not necessarily a permanent status for either a person or a place. A place that is currently haunted may not always be so. Conversely, just because your home and workplace are now ghost-free zones, there is no guarantee that they will always remain so.

Some ghosts and hauntings are incredibly tenacious. For example, the ghosts of Roman soldiers are still occasionally spotted roaming the English countryside where they battled centuries ago, but few ghosts are that ancient. As I have never heard or read of any place or person being haunted by the ghost of a prehistoric cave dweller, I presume that, like all forms of energy, ghosts eventually weaken and dissipate.

In the presence of a ghost or during an active haunting, observers will usually note predictable and distinguishable changes in their environment. Such changes often include a sudden, dramatic temperature drop that is very localized, though it may encompass a large area. Drafts, odours or noises—all of which are apparently sourceless—may also be present.

Despite the lack of agreement on what a ghost might be, ghosts exist in all cultures and have been noted throughout history. My own experience collecting ghost stories has taught me one other consistency: A paranormal encounter is a profoundly moving experience. I have yet to have a story told to me in a flippant or even a matter-of-fact way. Experiencing a ghost is clearly a deeply moving event in a person's life. Out of respect for this emotional factor, I have agreed to protect a contributor's anonymity when he or she has requested that I do so.

Not all of the paranormal phenomena in British Columbia are attributable to ghosts. The woods, waters and skies of this province are the settings for some equally interesting and thought-provoking stories of other kinds. A sampling of these reports makes up the last section of this book.

The narratives in this book are reports of real events, and we all know that life, as we live it, is anything but neat and tidy. As a result, these accounts sometimes tend to be more ragged than the stories that we may be used to reading. A fictional tale of a haunting will be structured, with a predictable presentation: a beginning, a middle and an end. The anecdotes recorded here often refuse to be that orderly. Sometimes they are merely fragments, which can be somewhat frustrating in a world so fond of neatness. We tend to find it more satisfying if any loose ends are bound up by the last sentence of a tale. However, in those cases where there hasn't been enough information to tell as a traditional story, the parts that are missing can be as provocative as the parts that remain.

This collection is not intended as an attempt to alter anyone's personal belief system with my convictions or explanations. My intent is to entertain and to possibly provoke thought in areas that you might otherwise not have considered exploring. Though I do not pretend to be an educator, if reading this book introduces you to facets of British Columbia's history or geography with which you were previously unfamiliar, then I am delighted.

For the most part, I have excluded the First Nations peoples' tales about spirits and the supernatural. Although these stories would definitely make a fascinating book, I am not qualified to write it.

If you have any additions to the stories contained in this volume, or personal experiences with the paranormal that you would like to share with me, please contact me through Lone Pine Publishing. I'd love to hear from you. In the meantime, do enjoy this unique look at some of British Columbia's folklore.

Chapter 1

HAUNTED HOUSES

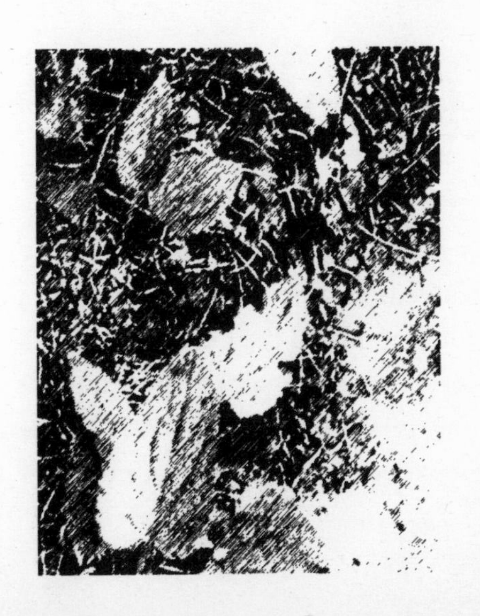

Our homes are extremely important to most of us. Whether home is a single room in a boarding house, a ranch, a city bungalow, or a condominium apartment in a downtown high-rise, we humans tend to develop strong emotional attachments to our homes. Perhaps, then, it shouldn't be too surprising that such an intimate, emotionally laden area is frequently also the site of paranormal activity.

After all, if on just about every evening of your life you saw your father reading the newspaper while sitting in a particular chair in a corner of the living-room, it would not be too surprising that, if he died, you might for some time afterward still occasionally think that you saw him there. Such a sighting really begs the question—does the image reside solely in the mind of the one perceiving it, or is a remnant of the man's spirit still enjoying the sports pages?

As evidenced by the following stories, though, there are certainly other ways in which our homes can become haunted.

Sidewalk Spectres

Sometimes it can be difficult to figure out why a particular location is haunted. At other times the reasons are very easy to understand; for example, in the following story from Coquitlam, which is just a short distance east of Vancouver.

It seems that in the summer of 1985 the owner of a small apartment house decided to fix the place up a bit. As part of his renovations, he purchased 130 stone slabs to use as a decorative pathway. What none of the tenants in the building knew at the time was that their pretty new sidewalk had been constructed from headstones, headstones removed when the land previously used by nearby Woodlands Hospital Cemetery was turned into a park.

The hauntings in the building began as soon as the new pathway was laid. For the most part, the displaced spirits were benign. They were, however, impossible to ignore as they wandered throughout the various suites in the apartment block.

One occupant was concerned enough to bring in a psychic, who confirmed that there were many spirits about the place, but reported that most of them were quite harmless, beyond their occasionally annoying ghostlike practical jokes, such as causing electrical devices to malfunction. The people whose homes were in this particular building had more than their share of those sorts of problems.

When gravestones were used to create a sidewalk, a small apartment building in Coquitlam became haunted.

Toasters would spontaneously heat up, lights would turn on and off, televisions would change channels—all when no one was near them.

Considerably more disturbing, however, were the ghost sightings. A woman whose name has only been recorded as "Mrs. Schneider" reported catching an occasional glimpse of the apparition of a child. In a nearby suite, however, the ghostly sightings were decidedly more threatening. There, children saw disembodied faces at night and, as they stared in horror, their beds would shake violently.

The building began to develop a well-deserved reputation as a haunted apartment house. Children from the neighbourhood became fascinated with the place until one pried up and turned over a piece of newly installed sidewalk. The youngsters fled as soon as they discovered that the particular piece of the walk that had been upturned was a headstone from a child's grave.

When the tenants expressed their displeasure at their landlord's decidedly odd sense of decorum, he relented, dug up the walk and created a more traditional one. Unfortunately, the haunting had already become well established and phantoms were seen in the building for many years afterward. By the early 1990s, the energy of the understandably agitated spirits had sufficiently subsided so that the dead and the living were at last able to share their accommoda-tion in peace.

Where's Waldo?

In the case of the British Columbia town of that name, the answer to that question is that what's left of it has been flooded over. However, according to local historian John Kinnear, "Some of Waldo does reappear ... at certain times of the year."

Located southwest of Fernie, Waldo was once a thriving community with two large sawmills, two hotels, a large school, stores, an Anglican church and a post office serving a population of seven hundred people. The town's decline began in the early 1920s when the first mill closed. Less than three years later, a fire destroyed virtually the entire town, leaving only six houses and the church standing.

In March 1972, the church was moved to nearby Baynes Lake, the remnants of the houses were demolished to the footings and the entire area was flooded, as a consequence of the construction of the Libby Dam and the subsequent filling of Lake Koocanusa. It is the foundations of those last remaining residences that reappear when the lake's water level dips.

All the houses were vacant long before they were destroyed—with the possible exception of a haunted house that may still have sheltered its ghost.

Like the town itself, the haunted house in Waldo was small, so small that it could have been a cosy and welcoming little place—but it was not. The place should have been a bargain, considering the small amount of rent that a landlord could demand in the isolation of a ghost town but, in terms of wear and tear on the tenants' nerves, one of Waldo's last occupied houses was anything but a good deal.

By the time a painter and his wife signed a short-term lease for the place, the paranormal activity in it had already driven out at least one tenant.

To help ensure that these new residents would at least have a chance of staying the season that they'd planned to, the landlord tried to explain as clearly as possible that unique rental conditions were attached to the property. He even went so far as to set down some decidedly peculiar guidelines—ones not recommended by any landlord and tenant act that I've ever heard of.

The couple was advised to always leave everything in the house just as they found it, no matter how inconvenient they might find it to be. Windows, for instance, that they found open should be left that way, even if doing so meant that the interior became uncomfortably chilly.

These unusual terms, combined with a definite feeling of unease while in one of the bedrooms, caused the new occupants to make inquiries of old-timers in the area. Before long, the couple had pieced together the reasons, not only for the former tenant's flight, but also for their own feelings of discomfort and for their landlord's strange directions. It seemed that the little house was widely believed to be haunted by the ghost of an elderly man who had once called the place home.

As they were intending to stay only for the summer, the couple decided to make the best of their strange housing bargain. In order to accommodate the never-seen, but frequently felt, presence, they were careful to abide by their landlord's advice. They left the furniture arranged exactly as it was when they first saw the place, even though that arrangement was not the one that they would have preferred. They never opened a window that they found closed nor closed one that was open.

The ghost, however, did not return their courtesies. It would frequently scatter books and papers about the place. Regardless of the mess, the couple always left everything as they found it. They learnt from experience that eventually the unseen hands that had caused the disorder would tidy the mess that they had made.

Despite the couple's efforts to be considerate, they were living in a haunted house and the ghost was apparently not going to let them forget it. Every evening, for instance, the clock on the mantel would chime. This situation in itself might not have been considered too unusual, except that the clock was only a shell. With no internal mechanism, the clock should have been incapable of making any sound. Furthermore, doors would suddenly slam closed with such force that all the windowpanes in the house would shake.

A few months later, as planned, the couple moved out of town, having lost little except (temporarily) their serenity. In return, they had gained a unique experience and a stockpile of stories with which to entertain their friends and family for years to come.

Knowing about the dam construction and its associated flooding, we do know the answer to the popular question, "Where's Waldo?" But we're still left to ponder where the ghost of Waldo could have gone.

Jason and Johnny

For a time during the 1970s, on a quiet street in North Vancouver, a most unusual friendship flourished. Unfortunately, this friendship had a lot of people concerned. You see, there was quite a difference in the ages of the two parties involved: Jason was just a little boy and Johnny was an adult. More importantly, Johnny was dead—had been for years.

But Jason was a lonely little fellow who wasn't in a position to be too picky about how and where he chose his friends. He was an only child of a single mother. Johnny came to see Jason regularly and was nice to the boy. Those qualifications were more than adequate for friendship as far as Jason was concerned.

The situation, however, was of grave concern to Jason's mother. Her son's relationship with Johnny had begun when the child was less than one year old. She first became aware that something extremely unusual was happening when she awoke to a strange sound coming from Jason's bedroom. At first she wasn't able to identify the sound but, after listening for a few seconds, she realized that the little boy was laughing out loud and hard.

The woman flew from her room into Jason's, presuming that the child was just dreaming. What she found gave her quite a start. Her son was sitting up in his crib and laughing hysterically. It was clear to Jason that there was someone else in the room with him—and that someone was bringing him no end of delight. Unfortunately, his mother could not see what her son could.

The laughing incident was only the beginning. These strange nightly occurrences became longer and more frequent. As a result, the child was missing out on badly needed sleep. "He was completely exhausted," she said of her son during that period.

One morning, after the visits had been going on for more than a year, Jason's mother discovered that the child's room had been trashed. "Bedding had been ripped, toys smashed and the legs of his bed had been torn off," the mother recalled. All of this destruction after a night when their house had been unusually quiet.

Much to her almost immediate regret, she punished Jason for having done so much damage to his room. She realized not long afterward that Jason could not possibly have been responsible for the mess. He was neither big enough, nor strong enough, to have wrought that much destruction. In retrospect, she realized that it was Johnny, not Jason, who had ravaged the room. And Johnny's antics were about to increase in frequency and intensity.

Over the next few years mother and son lived in chaos. Because he was visiting with his friend, Jason rarely slept between the hours of midnight and four in the morning. Jason's mother once watched in horror as a lampshade spun madly on its frame. No one was near the fixture at the time. The kitchen in the house became a focal point for ghostly activity. Cupboard doors flew open and closed. Drawers that were open would slam shut. A small appliance that had been hung on a wall dropped to the floor. In the living-room, an ornament that had been standing on a table flew toward a couch.

A friend from the neighbourhood who was visiting watched as Jason's mother emptied dirty water from a vase of flowers. Seconds later, she returned to the kitchen table to join her friend and found the vase once again filled with dirty water.

The mother's doctor thought that the woman had suffered a nervous breakdown when he heard her describe her living conditions. Fortunately there had been witnesses to these other occurrences as well, and so her friends and family were able to vouch for her sanity.

In addition to the water from the flowers reappearing, friends of Jason's mother had seen a hanging lamp swinging madly and pictures rocking back and forth, as well as the lampshade spinning. When a friend's daughter heard a disembodied growl, Jason's mother knew that she couldn't cope any longer.

Her discomfort increased considerably when she began to hear talk around the neighbourhood that their home stood on ground that had once been a burial site for the Burrard First Nations band. Feeling at a loss as to how to cope with the situation that she found herself in, the woman contacted both a member of the Vancouver Psychic Society and a person from the Burrard band.

The pair was able to confirm the woman's suspicions. Jason, they told her, was definitely being visited by the spirit of a band member whose body had, years ago, been interred somewhere very near her house. They were *not*, however, able to effect anything that would put a stop to the hauntings.

In the meantime, the strength of the visitor from beyond increased to the point that she could hear the ghost's deep, masculine voice. Jason, however, remained the only person who could actually *see* his friend. The lad described the entity as looking like "Daniel Boone in buckskins."

Eventually the haunting escalated and the mother contacted a psychologist to ask for help. In the doctor's opinion, the boy had been traumatized by his father's departure from the family and had created "Johnny" from "anthropomorphized psychic energy." It is doubtful that the psychologist's diagnosis brought Jason's mother much consolation. Whether the spirit had manifested from the Native burial ground or from her son's mental powers, it undeniably did exist. Not only had she heard a grown man's voice when she and Jason were alone in the house, but she and others had witnessed the mysterious whirlwinds of energy that an unseen force had blown through her house on numerous occasions.

This story is one of the many ghost stories that, for us, can have no definitive ending. There is apparently no information available about happened with this paranormally disturbed family since the summer of 1976, when Jason was a child of three. In many cases like this one, children temporarily lose their ability to perceive the supernatural and do not regain it until they reach puberty. If Jason followed this pattern, life for mother and son would have calmed down for a time. All that we can do is hope that Jason not only survived his childhood, but perhaps even thrived because of its unusual nature.

The Phantom Woodcutters' Ball

Legend has it that along Highway 3, in south-central British Columbia, almost exactly halfway between Trail and Grand Forks, there is a haunted abandoned moutainside home. The place is so haunted that few people have managed to spend an entire night there—not even on a dare. The ghosts that haunt this spooky old place are not only an industrious lot but appear to disapprove of unhealthy habits such as smoking cigarettes—although their apparent disapproval might just be another way of annoying any of the living who venture into their domain.

Neither the history of the old two-storey place, nor the identities of the ghosts, are known. Judging from their activities, it's probably safe to assume that they were woodcutters in the nearby mountain forests.

One man, recorded only as "Mr. JPL," came on a bet that he'd made with a friend. Confident that he would win both the bet and increased respect from the man, he selected a south-facing second-floor bedroom of the house and lay down with the expectation of sleeping calmly through the night. He began to drift off sometime around midnight. Just as JPL was losing consciousness, the door to the room that he'd chosen to sleep in swung open as though it had been kicked with great force—even though he was sure that he'd locked it before lying down.

Possibly figuring that his friend was playing a practical joke in an attempt to sway the odds of the bet, JPL immediately got up and searched the entire house. There was no sign that anyone, except himself, had been anywhere near the place. Not knowing whether to feel comforted or frightened by such a realization, the man went back to bed.

He'd no sooner put his head down again when he heard the sound of someone nearby splitting logs with an axe. JPL was really startled, because he had indeed noted a pile of logs near the house. As best he could remember, none had been split but, when he went outside to investigate the annoying sounds, he noticed that there was an axe propped up against the wall of the house and that some of the wood had now been cut.

Again he suspected that his friend was behind the prank, and so JPL took the axe, locked it in the house with him and went back to bed. Seconds later, the sounds of the woodcutting started up again. Determined to ignore the increasingly frightening sounds and the growing belief that the house was, as his friend had indicated, haunted, he lay in bed and listened to the axe crack against the logs. Finally, no longer able to contain himself, he ran down the stairs and out the front door. There, as neat as could be, was a stack of split wood.

JPL must have been a pragmatic man for, upon seeing this sight, he decided that the noises would now have to stop for there were no more uncut logs. Once again he made his way back to bed. This time he heard—not axes splitting logs—but chainsaws cutting down more trees. A little later the distinctive sounds of the axe began to echo in harmony with the saws.

The spirits in this abandoned mountainside house were really beginning to get wound up now. His bed began to shake violently and, coming from underneath it, JPL heard what he was sure was a vicious cat-fight. Seconds later, he heard someone knocking on his bedroom door. Relieved at the thought of some human company, the terrified man raced to the door, but was unable to open it. He pulled and pulled with all his might until whatever had been holding the door fast suddenly released its grasp, sending JPL flying across the room.

However, the worst was yet to come: as JPL landed in a frightened and sore heap, he was sure that he heard an evil-sounding laugh. In a last-ditch attempt to settle himself, JPL headed downstairs to have a cigarette. Just as he went to sit down, the chair that he'd been intending to sit on was yanked out from underneath him. As he landed on the floor for the second time in just a few minutes, he caught sight of his package of cigarettes lying nearby. For no apparent reason, they were soaking wet, and the sandwiches that he'd brought with him had been pulverized.

Angry now, and determined to catch the perpetrators, JPL rushed outside. He discovered nothing but beautiful mountain scenery heralding the beginning of another day. JPL had at least lasted through the night in the house and had therefore won the dare. He was more than ready to leave—and leave he did—but not before he noted that the woodpile outside the house was no longer split wood; it was inexplicably back the way it had been when he'd arrived the night before. Perhaps, even now, the phantom sawing and cutting are a nightly occurrence at that old haunted house in the mountains.

An Enigmatic Entity

Ghost stories are often puzzling. The following tale is even more puzzling than many others, because the family involved had been living in their house for nearly twenty-five years before it temporarily became haunted. Stranger still was the ghost's timing. The entity arrived just after there'd been a death in the family, but it was not the spirit of the family's recently deceased mother who came to haunt the place.

Because of the highly personal nature of this tale, the participants have requested that their identities be protected. For this reason I shall refer to the family as "the Millers" and restrict the description of the haunted house's location to merely stating that it was somewhere in British Columbia's Lower Mainland.

According to Mr. Miller, the first sign of a paranormal presence in the house came at night and consisted of "a terrifying sound . . . more like a voice than a noise," and yet, "it did not sound like a human voice." No one in the family had any idea what they'd heard. They just knew that it was loud enough to wake them up.

At first the frightened group wondered if their small dog could have been making the noises that they'd heard but, when they checked on their pet, they found it cowering silently in a corner. They could tell by his behaviour that he was as scared of the sound as they were.

On the second night, many of the ten people living in the suddenly haunted house thought that they heard the phantom utter either the word "why" or "die." On the third night, the Miller family moved out of the house, leaving only their dog and a tape recorder behind to hear the ghostly wails. Their experiment was a success—the audio tape recorded quite a cacophony. They recognized their dog's barking and, in addition to that noise, they heard another sound, which they described as sounding "like someone in deep agony." These disturbing noises were accompanied by footfalls heavy enough to make glasses resting on a table rattle audibly.

Not knowing what else to do, Mr. Miller called a pair of psychics to the house. They told the recently widowed man that they "felt a cold presence … like a cold shiver down your spine, like someone trying to grab hold of you." They saw the ghost of a man whom they described as being a "very confused entity" who was in pain.

The two sensitives were soon deeply moved by the spirit's torment. In order to accomplish their purpose, they kept praying and imagined themselves surrounded by a protective aura of white light. Over and over again, the psychics urged the lost soul to find his eternal rest. After a final moan, the ghost left, never to return, and the members of the Miller family were able to begin rebuilding their lives.

Historically Haunted in Victoria

The properties along Dallas Road in Victoria, with their unobstructed view of Juan de Fuca Strait in the foreground and the mountains of Washington State in the background, have long been acknowledged as among the most desirable pieces of real estate in Canada. If the scenery from these vantage points is a treat to behold today, we can only imagine how exquisite that same panorama must have been more than a hundred years ago.

The presence of such extraordinary natural beauty makes the long-ago events surrounding publisher George Nias even more poignant. Very soon after he built a large home at a certain Dallas Road address, the province's gold boom of the mid-1800s turned to bust and he lost the government contract to publish the provincial gazette, thrusting Nias into poverty. He abandoned his residence (some say without ever living in it) and fled to start life anew in Australia. The property, which stood on what used to be the Hudson's Bay Company's Beckley Farm, sat empty for some time. If there were any children in the neighbourhood, they might well have invented stories about the old Nias place being haunted because, after not too many months, it certainly looked the part. The once-grand structure quickly deteriorated and acquired a shabby, foreboding appearance.

However, it was another two years before the house actually became haunted. It was not only haunted, but apparently cursed as well. This part of the story began early in 1872, when the steamer

Prince Albert sailed into Victoria's harbour from San Francisco carrying immigrants to the island community. Victorians turned out in great numbers to welcome the ship and her passengers. Many of those standing on the dock that day had relatives on board whom they looked forward to helping settle in the growing community.

As the tiny, dark speck on the horizon became the discernible shape of a ship about to put into port, something of a party atmosphere pervaded those waiting. Sadly, the feelings of jubilation were soon dashed. The *Prince Albert* was making her way into the harbour with a yellow flag flying from her halyard. Everyone who saw the marker instantly understood its implication: souls stricken with smallpox were on board.

The ship docked only long enough for the Victoria-bound passengers to disembark—and to disgorge all the sick and dying. It didn't matter whether these latter pathetic folks had intended to go farther up-island or not; the rule was that if a passenger was ill, he or she was escorted off the ship at the next port of call. Though that precaution eliminated most of the anxiety for the *Prince Albert*'s crew, it certainly created an entirely new set of problems for the authorities in Victoria. Whatever were they to do with these patients? Eventually, someone suggested that they might be safely quarantined in the abandoned house on the Beckley Farm. And so they were.

As the ship's captain had done, city officials in charge of such matters flew a yellow flag from the seconded building. The banner would serve as a warning to all that, to use the euphemism of the day, this was a "pest house." The cold, hard truth was that entering the house would bring a visitor into certain contact with the killer disease that was then ravaging much of the world's population.

Initially there were seven patients isolated in Nias's former home, but an eighth victim disembarked from the *Prince Albert* on the ship's return trip from Nanaimo. This one was a member of the ship's crew. Soon the headcount at the large home was back down to seven, however, when on June 23, 1872, a youngster named Bertha Whitney succumbed to the disease. Her body was interred in an unmarked grave at Beckley Farm. Young Bertha's spirit was likely the first to haunt the property.

The sailor from the afflicted ship was the next to die. His remains were also hastily concealed on the grounds. The other six patients remained in the home until they were well again. Such statistics reflected a most unusual and impressive rate of recovery for a group attacked by this oft-lethal plague. Members of the surrounding community, however, focused on the original owner's flight from the area, followed by the two deaths, and determined that the place was somehow inherently evil. The building's reputation as an evil place spread quickly.

Once the six survivors recovered sufficiently to return to society, the makeshift pest house was abandoned for the second time in its short existence. Victorians, however, continued to give the empty place a wide berth, especially after dark.

The few brave souls who did travel past the house on Dallas Road at night were often witnesses to some frightening, and probably paranormal, sights. From the available descriptions, it would seem that the windows in the house were frequently alive with supernatural phenomena—ignes fatui, or ghost lights, as the mysterious orbs of illumination are now known.

Not surprisingly, the house at Beckley Farm remained unoccupied—by the living, anyway. No one from the area was interested in tempting fate by moving into the evidently haunted house.

About this time, however, an investor who claimed to be from San Francisco arrived in Victoria. Calling himself "Mr. P. Lackie," the nattily dressed man checked into the Angel Hotel. Over the next few weeks the newcomer said little about himself, until suddenly announcing to the hotel staff that his wife would soon be joining him from England and that he would, therefore, soon require more permanent accommodation. For reasons that are now unclear, the people at the hotel recommended that he consider residing at the former pest house.

Their direction proved fateful. Lackie soon fell victim to the Beckley Farm jinx. The second last time that the man was seen alive, he was observed in a heated argument near the possessed house. His opponent was a woman whom the witness had never seen before. The disagreement escalated until Lackie was observed recoiling from a vicious slap to the side of the head. When he was seen at the hotel later that day, the last time that anyone saw him alive, the man sported a badly bruised face.

Determining the order of the events that followed that appearance was initially somewhat confusing. On February 17, 1873, someone decided to explore the Beckley Farm property, but both the person's name and motivations for doing so have long been lost to history. These explorations no doubt ended the moment that they revealed the corpse of a shabbily dressed man. Police immediately assessed that it was a murder, as the man had been shot through the head at close range and no weapon could be found.

The confusion mounted with the Angel Hotel staff's discovery of a suicide note in one of their rooms. Although it no longer much mattered, the man whom they knew as "P. Lackie, from San Francisco" was actually P. Stocker, from Scotland. What did matter now was that he was dead. The note indicated that he intended to shoot himself in the head.

Further bewilderment erupted when a woman from Nanaimo was reported missing. Stranger still, her description exactly matched that of the woman seen slapping Lackie's (Stocker's) face. From

Victoria north, Island residents were stricken with fear. They were sure that there was a murderer loose.

It was several days before a series of events began to provide clues to all the mysteries. When a local street urchin tried to sell a gun to a shopkeeper, the man became suspicious and called the police. A quick check determined that the gun was identical to the one that killed the man found on the Beckley Farm property. The youngster and his relatives were immediately apprehended. Realizing that they were about to be accused of a crime much more heinous than the one that they'd actually committed, the little group hastily confessed their wrongdoings.

They had found the well-dressed suicide victim with his gun lying beside him. Determining that the corpse had no use for either his fine clothes or his gun, they relieved him of it all. Then, perhaps out of respect for the dead man's dignity, they dressed him in their old clothes and left him that way for the next person along to find. The house at Beckley Farm was living up to its malevolent reputation.

It would not last much longer, however. The haunted, possessed, jinxed and cursed house shortly afterward transformed itself into a pile of ashes in a mysterious and sudden blaze. Many people were sure that the ghost lights had started the fire. Nobody mourned the loss of the haunted house on Dallas Road.

Unbelievably, the evil forces were not yet completely spent. One of the *Prince Albert*'s stricken passengers who'd been isolated at the Beckley Farm house had recovered fully and was moving on with her life. Toward that end, she sent the dress that she'd worn on the voyage to a seamstress's shop to be altered slightly. According to a May 2, 1953, newspaper report, the dressmaker and several members of her family contracted smallpox from the soiled and infected dress. Their deaths were the final ones recorded as having been associated with the haunted house on Dallas Road.

Bedtime Party

An excellent example of retrocognition took place during the early 1930s, at a party in a recently renovated West End Vancouver house, where the event was witnessed by a room full of people.

To learn the background of this intriguing story, we must go back to the early 1900s, when a man and his wife purchased a small parcel of land in what is now the West End and proceeded to build their home on it. They moved in as soon as the house was completed. Neighbours later reported that the newcomers were rather an odd pair, in that the woman was extremely outgoing but the man was a virtual recluse. No one in the area had a chance to learn much more than that about the homeowners, because the woman died just six months later. The bereaved husband hastily sold the place and moved away.

No more is known about the place between that time and 1931, when it was purchased by a young couple. Initially the two were delighted with their real-estate investment exactly as it was and they did not plan to make any changes to the interior layout. The master bedroom was on the main floor, which they felt was a convenient arrangement.

From their first night in that room, however, they felt uneasy. When the feeling did not leave, the pair decided that some renovations would be necessary after all. They decided to sleep in another bedroom and to enlarge the living-room to include most of what had been the original master bedroom.

It was not long before the changes had been completed. The couple was so pleased with the way that their home looked now that they decided to invite their friends over for a party. The celebration got off to a successful start. According to a woman who had been a guest that night, everyone was enjoying themselves in the newly enlarged living-room until "precisely 11 o'clock." She recalled the room becoming "unaccountably cold" at that moment and described a "whirlwind of nothingness" suddenly manifesting in the part of the room that had been the bedroom.

"Then out of the whirlwind slowly emerge[d] a massive four-poster bed of richest rosewood upon which a woman was lying, clearly at the point of departure from this life. Her eyes were fixed in fear and horror upon the indistinct figure of a man sitting in a Victorian chair at her bedside," she continued.

One of the guests, a neighbour who had lived in the area a long time, shouted out that he recognized the apparitions. He identified them as the couple who had built the place, the home's original owners.

The images didn't stay long, but they did succeed in bringing the house-warming party to an abrupt and early end. Agreeing to tell no one of the paranormal event that they had just witnessed in their friends' home, the guests quickly dispersed.

Despite all the effort that they had put into the place, the new owners now realized that they could never be comfortable staying there and immediately listed their home for sale. The couple was relieved that the place sold quickly. As they wanted to be completely clear of anything associated with the haunted house, they even arranged to sell all their newly purchased furniture, draperies and rugs.

The woman who provided the account of the party and the manifestation of the bed and the apparitions attended the auction where her friends' belongings were to be sold. Perhaps she was interested in purchasing some of the items herself, for she inspected the articles carefully. The living-room rug was especially attractive to her. Her interest quickly turned to horror, however, when she discovered that at one end of the carpet there was a rectangular arrangement of "four well-worn indentations." It looked "exactly as though some heavy piece of furniture," perhaps a large, four-poster rosewood bed, "had rested there for a matter of months."

Most of the people who attended that house-warming party have presumably by now gone on to their own final reward—without ever having publicly identified themselves as participants in this incident of retrocognition.

And the haunted house? As is usually inevitable in the case of such valuable real estate, the house was demolished and a large apartment building now stands where it once did.

It would be interesting to know if any of the tenants have ever seen anything unexplainable anywhere in any of the suites.

A Phantom Roommate

Small, nondescript apartment buildings dot this country's urban landscapes. Although many of these multiple-family residences were constructed in the 1950s, they continue to provide adequate accommodation today for those living on a limited budget.

One particular apartment block on West 12th Avenue in Vancouver offered one important "added extra"—choosing to live at this address meant that you might have an occasional ethereal visitor. No one has ever been able to figure out who the ghost may have been when he was alive, but at least three residents know that, as a ghost at least, he was a companionable sort of fellow.

After a period of adjustment, two men who shared a suite in the haunted building came to quite enjoy the spirit's presence in their lives. Initially they had no idea what was causing an apparently sourceless shadow to occasionally appear, and they were frightened by it. Once they realized that the apparition would do them no harm, the pair became quite accepting, and even welcoming, of their "guest." Once that acceptance had occurred, the phantom sometimes also manifested as that strange sensation of not being alone, when reason says that no one else is in the room.

The pair of renters might not always have been able to see the phantom's form, but they could hear him as he settled into one or another of the chairs in the living-room. They soon got into the habit of offering pleasantries to their invisible visitor in order to acknowledge his arrival. Some months later, and for reasons completely unrelated to the ghost, the men moved on. They left the haunted apartment behind but never forgot the entity, nor the time that they had spent with him.

Many years after leaving that apartment, one of the men happened to meet a woman who had also lived in the building. She too had stories to tell—stories that were eerily similar to his. It seemed that the phantom travelled from one suite to another, socializing, to the best of his ghostly ability, as he went.

A Wicked Wraith

Malicious poltergeist activities took place during August 1938, in a house somewhere on Uplands Road in the Oak Bay suburb of Victoria. The exact address of this temporarily haunted house and the full names of those who resided in it at the time of the haunting are recorded in my files. However, out of consideration for the home's current owner—who probably has no idea what once happened on his valuable property—I have minimized the number of clues as to its identity. I might not have been so careful to do so if this ghost story was not one of the most venomous that I've ever been told.

For the reason that I mentioned, the identification of the cast of unfortunate characters in this tale will be limited to first names. Harry was a prominent lawyer who had just married Edith, an accomplished pianist ten years his junior. After the honeymoon, Harry would not need to make much in the way of adjustment to married life. Not only was the couple moving to the large house where Harry had been raised, but even the family's loyal maid, Mary, had happily agreed to stay on.

Edith was looking forward to using the hours while her husband was at work to settle into her new home; a process that included developing some rapport with Mary. Although she couldn't pinpoint exactly why, Edith felt an atmosphere of hostility in the large, luxurious home. In fact, nearly forty years after she moved in, Edith was quoted as having known right from the start that "hate was abroad in the house." As there were certainly no bad feelings between her and Harry, Edith deduced that she was sensing Mary's resentment at the arrival of "another woman" into the household.

Wanting to resolve the situation, Edith was prepared to accept Mary on any terms that the maid wished to establish. But, as it would later turn out, it was not Mary's energy that she was sensing. However, it would take her awhile to realize that the malicious goings-on to come were not Mary's doing, but the actions of an evil poltergeist.

Shortly after Edith moved in, strange things began to happen. Initially she found pictures on the wall that she knew had been hanging straight just moments before were suddenly askew. An annoying occurrence, yes, but far from a threatening one. The evil spirit was gaining strength, however, for it then toppled a vase of fresh-cut flowers.

The next act of phantom vandalism was considerably more serious. Edith could hardly believe her eyes when she found the upholstery on her newly purchased chesterfield had been slashed, as if with a knife. Devastated by what she took to be Mary's intentional meanness, she confronted the maid and accused her of perpetrating the destruction.

Expecting the servant to be defensive, Edith was dumbfounded at the woman's near-hysterical reaction. Not only did Mary deny ever having damaged anything in the house, she explained that she had purposely *not* repaired the destruction so that the bride would be sure to notice it. The malicious acts were meant for Edith's attention, Mary was sure.

Now, more confused than ever, Edith pressed the woman to explain herself. "You'll have to ask the master, Madam," was all that the servant would reveal before rushing from the room.

Presently, the phone rang. Harry was calling to say that he'd be working late at the office.

"Have dinner yourself, my love," he admonished, "and please don't wait up for me. It may be past your bedtime before I get home."

With great effort, Edith kept her voice controlled throughout the conversation and, as a result, was sure that Harry would have no idea how distressed she was. After a moment's consideration, Edith decided that perhaps a few extra hours alone with Mary might not be a bad thing after all. It might allow her the time to get to the bottom of the disturbing situation in her new home.

Toward this end, she called the woman back into the living-room. Speaking as kindly and gently as she possibly could, Edith tried to assure Mary that she did want the two of them to be on good terms.

"I don't hate you, Madam," the maid replied. "I'm content with my place and don't want to leave. It's Mr. Harry, Madam. He must stop hating. He counters hate with hate. I've told him many times that he must change his ways but he's stubborn and won't listen. This evil that you've seen and felt around this house is hate from beyond the grave. Even the strength of the Mister's hate can never overpower that. He needs to meet this hate with forgiveness or there will never be peace in the house."

Mary's impassioned explanation was interrupted by a second phone call. The maid left the room to answer the persistent ringing and, when she came back, it was clear to Edith that the woman was even more upset. It seemed that Mary's sister had been involved in an accident and was asking for her.

Something in the maid's protestations of innocence in regards to the unusual goings-on must have convinced Edith of her sincerity. And, although she knew that she'd have to let Mary go to her sister, she realized that she was dreading being alone in the house with the evil presence.

As she hurried away, Mary reinforced the importance of Edith convincing her husband that he must stop hating.

"Just remember, Madam, none of this will stop until he's forgiven the person he's hating," Mary reiterated as she fled from the house.

"Who? Who must he stop hating and forgive?" Edith shouted as the door slammed.

"He'll know," came the reply from the other side of the closed door.

Thoroughly confused and quite frightened, Edith sat at the kitchen table eating the sandwich that she would call dinner. Food might calm her, she reasoned. However, just moments later she felt unseen icy fingers groping at her. She instantly realized that the evil in the kitchen with her was more than she was capable of counteracting.

Fearing for her life, she bolted from the kitchen to the apparent safety of the living-room. This room looked so calm and serene that she felt foolish at having been nearly hysterical just moments earlier. She sat at the piano and laid her hands on the familiar arrangement of keys. Playing always soothed her nerves.

A second later, she glanced up. Had that shadow always been in the corner of the room? She tried to convince herself that it had, but failed. The evil chortle that the dark presence then emitted was more than she could endure. Screaming senselessly, Edith began to pound out chord after chord on the piano.

Soon she realized that the shadow in the corner was lightening somewhat. Her chords became less harsh, more melodic—until she found her fingers playing the familiar notes of a favourite sonata. The sense of the vile presence was now all but gone.

Edith played on until she suddenly felt foolish at having allowed herself to become so frightened over what had clearly been nothing at all. Wanting to refresh herself for Harry's return home, she got up from the piano, intending to make her way to the dressing table in their bedroom.

The evil spirit that had been driven back by the music seized this moment of silence and vulnerability. Its essence revitalized. Moments later, the phantom was again strong enough that Edith sensed it. She could no longer fight. Collapsing onto the nearest chair, her last fully conscious thought was whether the manifestation of hatred was possibly Mary herself, or whether the maid's warnings had been sincere.

Regaining consciousness moments later, Edith remembered that Harry had a gun in the house. She rose to search for it but was soon driven back by the sheer malevolence that surrounded her. As she watched, the energy began to take on a clearer and clearer form until the image of an angry woman stood in front of her. And that woman was not Mary, but someone whom Edith was sure she'd never seen before.

Finding Harry's gun was pointless, the terrified woman realized. Firearms would do no good against this enemy. It was not of this world. Edith could see the apparition clearly and yet she could also see right through it. Uttering menacing, incomprehensible sounds, the evil image made its way toward Edith, who stood frozen in terror.

Hands extended threateningly, the manifestation was almost within reach of strangling her victim when the front door burst open. Harry had arrived home at last.

"Lois!" he screamed, with evident hate.

It was then that Edith recalled the maid's wise counsel.

"Don't curse her, Harry, whoever she is. Hating her will only strengthen her powers. Forgive her Harry, for whatever wrongs she did to you," Edith implored.

"Forgive her? How could I? This woman stood me up at the altar and then spread vicious untruths about me throughout our entire circle of friends. How could I possibly forgive her?" Harry demanded.

"You must, Harry, if we're to have any peace in our lives, you must forgive this woman's soul," Edith countered.

"All right, Lois. I don't hate you any more. Just go. Go from our lives. Leave us alone. Go on to your final rest," the man ordered.

The ghost stood in shimmering—but poised and malevolent—stillness.

"Forgive her, Harry. Forgive her," Edith repeated.

For a moment there was silence, then Harry's demeanour softened noticeably.

"Edith is right. All this hate has no place in this home now. You wronged me, Lois, but I have no reason now to keep hating you. I forgive you and beg you to go on to your final reward and let me get on with my life. You and I have no more need of each other," he concluded.

As the last of Harry's words hung in the air, the atmosphere began to lighten until the evil spirit had completely dispersed, never to return to that posh home on Uplands Road.

Chapter 2

GHOSTLY GHOST TOWNS

Despite the implications in the term "ghost town," there are probably many abandoned communities that are not haunted. Verification one way or the other is, by definition, difficult because there is no one there to report on the presence (or absence) of ghosts. Thankfully for ghost lovers everywhere, many other ghost towns are haunted, and there is anecdotal evidence to prove it.

Well-Haunted Barkerville

Barkerville, in east-central British Columbia, is a preserved ghost town, a place where visitors can meander through the streets of history. Much of the old town remains standing, haunted and available to be explored. For the ghost hunter, that means only one thing—lots of haunted buildings to investigate.

Like many of the western towns that were established in the 1800s to serve the needs of those chasing instant wealth in the various gold rushes, Barkerville has an intriguing history. In the mid-1800s, Billy Barker, an English sailor, jumped ship and made his way to the Interior of British Columbia. There, along with hundreds of others, he searched for the golden mother-lode. Unlike many others, Billy Barker did strike it rich. As a matter of fact, he found a great deal of gold and became wealthy beyond his wildest imaginings.

Barkerville sprang up, just south and east of Prince George, to supply Barker and the other miners in the area. The town flourished for a number of years and was known far and wide as one of the most law-abiding towns in the West. Such peacefulness was not a result of the citizens' inherent goodness, but simply the town's inaccessible location. Barkerville is so out of the way that if a crime was committed, all that was necessary to corner the perpetrator was to seal off the few roads leading out of town. As a result, Barkerville wasn't nearly as rowdy a place as most mining towns. Despite its placid past, Barkerville was haunted already even when it was a burgeoning community.

Today, it is still home to at least three ghosts. But it was a ghostly appearance during the town's heyday that was the most remarkable manifestation. Wellington Moses operated Barkerville's barber shop. With very little effort beyond opening the shop, he created a successful business and became friendly with many of his customers—including Morgan Blessing, a wealthy and flamboyant American. Blessing had not been raised with money and, liking to show off what he had acquired, wore distinctive gold jewellery made from nuggets that he had mined.

In no time at all, Blessing and Moses became fast friends. Soon they met a third man, James Barry, an unscrupulous fellow who saw the friendship between Moses and Blessing as an opportunity to enrich his own pocketbook. Barry planned on, and succeeded in, causing conflict between the two friends. Soon tensions ran so high that, on their way back from a trip to the Coast, Moses left the other two and went on ahead.

Not long after the barber had settled back into his home and shop in Barkerville, he heard that James Barry was also back in town. Morgan Blessing, however, was not. Interestingly, Barry's personal wealth had grown astronomically in just a few short days. Wellington Moses was deeply concerned by this turn of events but, beyond his own suspicions, there was no evidence that anything illegal had occurred. After all, Morgan Blessing was an adult; if he'd decided to move on to another town, rather than return to Barkerville, it was really no one's business but his own. By the same token, James Barry might have come by his new wealth honestly. There was no evidence to the contrary—so far.

Several weeks later, Moses was shocked to see his old friend Morgan Blessing struggling in through the front door of his barber shop. The man looked much the worse for wear. His clothes were ripped and muddy, his complexion pasty, his eyes bloodshot. Barely able to make his way to the barber chair, Blessing indicated to Moses that he wanted a shave.

Speechless with both relief at seeing Blessing again, and concern for the man's obvious distress, Moses set about preparing to give the man the shave that he'd requested. He wrapped Blessing's face in a warm, moist towel before turning to sharpen the razor that he planned to use. When, just a few seconds later, Wellington Moses glanced back at his friend, he saw a sight that he'd never forget—the towel that he'd placed on his friend's face was soaked with blood. Seconds later the man's image vanished. Only the bloodstained towel remained. To Moses, it was clear evidence that a foul and fatal deed had been committed and needed to be avenged. Despite this apparent plea from beyond the grave, there was little that Moses could do to prove that James Barry had murdered and robbed Morgan Blessing.

Several weeks later, Blessing's remains were found, with a single bullet hole in the back of his head. It was now clear that he had been murdered. But the body alone did nothing to implicate James Barry in any way. Barry's connection with the crime went unproven until a Barkerville woman began showing off an unusual pin, explaining that Barry had given it to her. By the middle of the following summer,

James Barry had been accused, tried, found guilty of murder and hanged.

Presumably Morgan Blessing's spirit found solace in this justice, for his ghost was never seen in Barkerville again.

Had Mr. Blessing cared to drop in on Barkerville a second time after his death, he would not have been lonely for, even today, there are ghosts in the town. Madame Fannie Bendixon still looks out a second-floor window of the building that housed her saloon. The image is so lifelike that visitors assume that the manifestation is one of the site's historic interpreters. Not so. There is never any living person on the second floor of the old building because, since the staircase collapsed many years ago, there is no way to get to that level. From descriptions of the oft-seen apparition and records of Fannie Bendixon's appearance, it is clear that the woman's spirit has stayed behind to keep a watchful eye on what was once her business.

Another haunted building in Barkerville is much more puzzling. Barkerville's Theatre Royal of today is not an original building but merely a replica. Despite this lack of authentic history, the place is definitely home to ghosts. Footfalls are routinely heard making their way across the stage floor, when no one can be seen anywhere near that area. Furthermore, isolated pockets of cold air, which are generally acknowledged as indicative of the presence of a spirit in a building, have been noted throughout the theatre.

Music has been heard coming from the theatre's speakers—even when no power was connected to them—and, during productions in the theatre, apparitions have turned up on the stage, especially frequently at stage left. That's where performers report seeing the image of a man, dressed in formal attire from the nineteenth century. In the split second that it takes the startled people to realize that there shouldn't be anyone in that location, the image vanishes. Over the years, that particular ghost's appearance has been reported

The theatre is only one of the haunted buildings in the haunted ghost town of Barkerville.

with amazing consistency. He's described by all who've seen him as sporting a top hat, tails and a moustache. No one knows who the long-deceased dandy might be—just that when he's seen, he's always in the same location and attire. Perhaps before and after he makes his appearances to the living, he relaxes with Fannie at the saloon, or with the town's phantom piano player, who is yet another ghostly resident of Barkerville.

And so, among ghost towns, Barkerville is something of an exception in that more than just the buildings have been preserved—even the spirit of the place lives on.

Michel's Manifestations

Geological processes have invested the mountains of British Columbia with a cache of precious metals and valuable minerals. Mining those resources has led to the establishment of communities where the miners, and sometimes their families, can live. But what happens to these towns when the sought-after metals and minerals either run out or become too expensive to profitably mine? Many of those mining towns become ghost towns, some with colourful ghost stories to relate.

Michel, near the town of Sparwood in the southeastern part of the province, is just such a place. The lively little town that existed from the 1800s to the 1960s is now a mere shadow of its former self. A haunted hotel is one of the few remaining buildings.

Legend has it that, during the Great Depression of the 1930s, the owner of the only hotel in town became so fed up with drifters staying in his establishment and then not being able to pay their bills that he actually hanged one non-paying customer. Having paid the ultimate price for his accommodation, George, that poor and punished customer, has decided to stay on at the hotel into eternity.

Sometimes George's ghost can still be seen sitting in a chair at a spot in the hallway on the third floor outside where his room once was. At other times he's more active, causing candles or flashlights carried by warmer-blooded guests to extinguish as they pass the door to his former room. It was probably George's ghost too that once would not allow a tourist to make her way down the hall. The phantom just stubbornly refused to let her pass.

There is at least one other resident spectre on the third floor, making it difficult to always know for sure which ghost is up to what mischief. This second spirit belongs to a woman who killed herself while staying at the hotel. Staff blame her when they hear water running on the third floor. Sceptics should note that a more pragmatic explanation cannot be offered—there is no plumbing on that level of the hotel.

Many people think that a number of other spirits reside at the Michel Hotel, but the identities of these additional ghosts are unknown.

Chapter 3

HAUNTED MUSEUMS

A museum is a remarkable institution: it is a single place where items from many disparate sources and histories are brought together and preserved. Each artifact has its own story to tell and many of those stories are ghost stories.

Charlie's Presence

It should not be surprising to discover that museums and art galleries are often haunted. After all, they are caches of artifacts, each piece with its own history. Sometimes, though, it's the history of the building that houses those artifacts that accounts for the museum's haunted status.

In Greenwood, a small city west of Grand Forks in the south of the province, that was certainly the case. The local museum now has its own building but, for the fifteen years from 1967 to 1982, it was housed in the old courthouse building—the haunted old courthouse building.

History tells us that in July 1915 a prisoner being kept in a basement cell hanged himself. It is said that the man's restless spirit has roamed the building ever since. Half a century later, his presence was so real to the museum employees who worked with the ghost around that they gave him a name. They called him Charlie.

No one on staff had any reason to fear Charlie. His antics were, at worst, merely a nuisance to the living. A certain mannequin, however, was clearly on Charlie's "hit list." One day an employee went to check on the sounds of water running in a supposedly deserted back room. He found the dummy's head floating in a bathtub full of water.

After turning off the taps and letting the water out of the tub, the employee dried off the head and reattached it to the mannequin's body, presuming that the incident was closed. Apparently it was not, because some days later the curator arrived at work to find that the mannequin's head had been knocked off the body. It now lay across the room on the floor—smashed to bits.

Charlie's presence was once credited with frightening an employee when she was alone in the building. On this occasion he smashed an ashtray. As he never did anything like that again, it's possible that he simply didn't approve of smoking. Apart from these antics, the ghost usually made his presence known by simply walking around the building and occasionally thumbing through racks of newspapers.

Charlie's earthly life may have been cut short, but it seems that he's making sure that his "hereafter" lasts for a long time.

Persistent Presences

World-renowned artist Emily Carr was born at her parents' estate on Victoria's Government Street in 1871, not far from the site of George Nias's haunted house (see "Historically Haunted" in Chapter 1). Both the woman herself and Emily Carr House have given rise to some intriguing ghost stories.

In her autobiography Emily notes that she was a "contrary" child who did not seek out the company of other children. Instead, she preferred to spend her time with the farm animals on the property or simply roaming about alone.

In common with many solitary children, young Emily adopted an "invisible friend" who often accompanied her on her explorations. This companion was so real to Emily that, years later as an adult, she reflected on the possibility that her companion was actually a ghost, and not just the product of her own imagination. "I always wondered if it was the spirit of a young boy who joined me," she attested.

The Carrs' original land has since been subdivided. What remains with the house today is only a fraction of the original size, but the family home still stands. Some people believe it to be haunted. My own experience while visiting Emily Carr House has made me one of those people.

I'd looked forward to visiting the house from the moment that I'd planned my trip to Victoria. Not only was I hoping for a ghost story, but my interest in Canadian art history made Emily Carr House, at 207 Government Street, a "must see." Seconds after I walked into the house, I asked a staff member whether or not it was haunted. She smiled enigmatically and suggested that I tour the house and come back to report my impressions. Even though I don't claim to be psychically sensitive, I accepted the challenge and began to explore various rooms.

I thoroughly enjoyed poking about the main floor, but sensed nothing out of the ordinary. As soon as I climbed the stairs, however, I felt uncomfortable, as though I was intruding into someone else's space. Although my urge was to escape the sensation by retreating to the main floor, I'd waited a long time to visit Emily's birthplace and was determined to at least complete my tour.

Emily's parents' bedrooms are on display and look as they would have when the family was living in the house. Although the public is

Emily Carr House and the area surrounding it have long been home to spirits.

invited to walk right into Mrs. Carr's bedroom, I found that I wasn't able to. A sense that it was someone else's personal space was just too strong and I went back downstairs immediately.

After waiting a moment to compose myself, I approached the woman I'd spoken to earlier. She smiled and acknowledged that Emily Carr House is indeed haunted, but not by Emily. It is the ghost of Emily Carr's mother that has remained. Apparently, as a youngster, Emily was afraid to climb the staircase at night. To ease the child's fears, her mother used to stand at the top of the stairs while the child made her way up. That anecdote certainly explained the protective presence that I had detected as I climbed the stairs.

Emily's mother's bedroom is the only other area of the house thought to be haunted. Although Mrs. Carr died in 1886, her spirit has not entirely left her former home.

But what of the spirit of the artist herself? Although her ghost has never been seen in her childhood home, her spirit hasn't completely left the city where she spent much of her life. The ghost of Emily Carr is often seen at nearby St. Ann's Academy, a historic site that previously served as a girls' school and as a convent. In one such incident in 1992, Victoria resident Greg Hartnell saw her image and his sighting was later confirmed by a second witness.

James Fry, a cable television producer, had previously seen Carr's apparition in November 1991, while scouting for filming locations. The encounter took place in the early evening. Fry watched in fascination as the ghostly image appeared at a window in the otherwise vacant St. Ann's. Apparently open-minded to the concept of ghosts, the producer expressed interest in possibly interviewing the ghost on television. Unfortunately, the spirit did not cooperate.

A year earlier, retired businessman Arthur Knight reported to the newspaper that he'd seen "two hooded figures at St. Ann's just as dawn was breaking." The man had the good fortune to have a camera with him at the time and quickly snapped a shot that later confirmed his observations. It would seem that in death, at least, Emily Carr is not alone.

The Haunted Hall

In the Fraser Valley city of Chilliwack, the museum is housed in the old city hall, not far from where the haunted house on Williams Street once stood, (see "Portrait Possessed" on p. 138). The grand old building, constructed in 1912, routinely held prisoners awaiting trial. In 1928, a man charged with the possession of opium was thrown into a cell with another prisoner. While the man already staying in the cell was asleep, the new arrival stole his belt and used it to strangle himself. His tragic spirit has been in the building ever since.

The entity can be heard walking about when the rest of the building is known to be empty. The back door will clearly be heard opening and closing when no one is near it. Perhaps the long-deceased prisoner is enjoying in death the freedom denied to him in life. There is no longer any lock in the world that can hold him. He's free now to leave and re-enter any building whenever he pleases.

The Blue Lady

Some called her "Sophia" and others used the more general descriptor "the Blue Lady." Regardless of what name they knew her by, those who worked in the museum in the sunny Okanagan city of Penticton readily acknowledged the ghost's presence.

The apparition was once actually sighted standing beside a

display. At other times, however, witnesses saw only a vague blue haze or heard the rustling of the skirts of her period costume. They reported feeling a female presence in the room—a feeling that their eyesight could not confirm. There were also sudden, unaccounted-for pockets of cold air felt throughout the building, as well as the sounds of footsteps when there was no one visible.

The haunting came to an abrupt end in 1992, when the staff examined a box that had been stored in the building. Writing on the outside of the carton indicated only that the contents had been "found on the east side of the river." The investigators were understandably concerned when they discovered that the articles inside were bones—human bones. The proper authorities were notified immediately. A closer examination revealed that the bones were from not just one skeleton but that they had come from two women and one man.

Much to the staff's collective relief, the spectre has not been detected in the Penticton Museum since that box of bones was removed from the property.

Penticton is not the only place in British Columbia with a "Blue Lady." There is also an entity of that colour in Victoria.

This Blue Lady has been seen at the Point Ellice House on Pleasant Street, which was bought by Magistrate and Mrs. Peter O'Reilly in 1868. One of their daughters, Kathleen O'Reilly, never married and resided in this home for her entire life—and apparently for at least the first thirty years following her death.

Point Ellice House, no longer a private home, is now a museum and tearoom operated by the provincial government. Kathleen's spirit hasn't been seen too often since the house passed out of her descendents' hands but, in years gone by, unsuspecting visitors to the house have sometimes enjoyed a guided tour led by an extremely knowledgeable and gentle woman wearing an old-fashioned blue dress (and bearing a remarkable resemblance to Kathleen). When their very thorough tour was over, the guests were most incredulous to find that the only guide working that day was busy with another group and looked very different from the woman who'd so proudly shown them around.

After the ghost of Kathleen took two men on a tour of Point Ellice House one day, they reported that she followed them out to the street and on down the road before simply disappearing.

A Spirited Museum

The pretty Vancouver Island community of Ladysmith, located north of Duncan and south of Nanaimo, is home to the privately operated Black Nugget Museum. According to owner Kurt Guilbride, the building that houses the museum is "well over one hundred years old." It began life as the Miners' Hotel, in what was then a mining boom town. In that incarnation the place saw more than its fair share of action, including at least one murder. Perhaps as a result of this lively past, the building is now thought to be haunted.

One museum visitor enjoyed a lively conversation with the ghost of an elderly Native woman. The guest, who was a spirit channeller, spoke at length with the presence, whose body's remains are an exhibit in the museum.

Trinkets that Kurt Guilbride displays facing in one direction are regularly found facing another—even though no one's been near them. In addition, disembodied footsteps are sometimes heard on the staircase. It is clear that, at the Black Nugget Museum, the past has really been brought to life.

Is the Gallery's Ghost Gone?

The province has had at least one other haunted art gallery, this one in the city of Victoria. The personable and popular Theo Hare was the curator of the Norfolk Gallery on Broad Street until his death in the 1950s. When a new administrator, Katie Bloomfield, took over responsibility for the displays, she soon recognized that Mr. Hare had not really left the building.

At first, Bloomfield simply felt her predecessor's presence. The effect on her was predictable: she had the feeling that the hair on the back of her neck was standing up. As she became more used to being in the haunted building, the ghost's strength increased and she could often make out a misty form of a man's shape hovering near the room that had been Theo Hare's office.

After a few years, for reasons not related to the entity, Katie Bloomfield sold the gallery to a couple named Chris and Alma Phillips. The couple had a four-year-old boy. As is often the case, the child could see the ghostly image much more clearly and much more frequently than his parents could. It was also typical that the parents were concerned about Hare's visits from beyond, whereas the boy was accepting and even welcoming of the occasional guest.

The Phillips family left the Broad Street address in the early 1960s. The building is no longer an art gallery and, as far as has been reported, is also no longer haunted. Perhaps the ghost's interest in the building finally died out when the art displays left.

The Haunted Tod House

Anyone who knew him might well have named John Tod as the most unforgettable character that they had ever met. Tod was, undeniably, a strong and unique personality. As a young man he had left a safe, secure home in Scotland for whatever adventures Canada might have to offer.

Tod was a trader for the Hudson's Bay Company and most of his activities during his life were enmeshed with business. Along the way he married several times. Some say that he had four wives; others maintain that he married as many as seven times. It is known that Tod sired a total of ten children with the various Mrs. Tods.

When he retired, John Tod chose to do so in Victoria. He purchased 186 hectares (460 acres) of prime real estate just a short distance from Oak Bay on which to build his spacious retirement home. Land was a lot less expensive then, for the year was 1851.

John Tod died at home in 1882, at the age of ninety-four. He was an agnostic who had given specific orders that no funeral be held in his honour. Sophia, his wife at that time, was a devout Christian and couldn't bring herself to comply with her husband's wishes. She had her husband interred with a full Christian ceremony. Supernatural activity in Tod House began shortly afterward.

Dishes would rattle noisily in the cupboards. Jars hung from hooks on the wall would rock back and forth. Doors that were open would slam closed. Doors that were closed would swing open. Clothes hung on racks would be flung about. An unoccupied rocking chair rocked back and forth as though someone was sitting in it. Footsteps and indistinct voices were heard throughout the place.

Colonel and Mrs. Evans, who bought the house in 1944, may have been shown just how strongly John Tod—or his ghost—felt about Christian festivals when they decorated their newly purchased home for Christmas. They awoke on Christmas Day to find the holiday decorations that they had lovingly set out "stripped from the walls and the tree and piled neatly in the centre of the living-room floor."

The Evanses soon discovered other inconveniences associated with living in the big old place. There was one room that no one liked to go into. Privately, the Evanses called it "the eerie room." They felt that it was constantly and inexplicably colder than the rest of the house. On one occasion, guests who had been put up in that bedroom hurriedly left before dawn. They had seen an apparition—a particularly unnerving apparition. To them had appeared an image of a dark-haired woman bound in chains and leg-irons, gesturing soundlessly for help.

Evidently, John Tod's spirit was not the only one prowling about their home. In another incident involving the eerie room, the window, which had been nailed closed for some time, crashed out of its frame onto the lawn below when no one (visible) was near it. The mess left behind is said to have looked as though someone had tried to escape from the room.

The Evanses' suspicions about there being another ghost at large were confirmed in 1952. Workers whom they'd hired to convert the home's heating system to oil made a grisly discovery. There, over two metres (seven feet) below ground level in the excavation that the labourers had dug for the oil tank, lay a human skeleton.

Examination confirmed that these remains were of a Native woman. Her body had decomposed quickly, probably as a result of liberal amounts of lime being thrown into her makeshift grave. John Tod's wife before Sophia had been a dark-haired woman. Local historians recalled being told that she had gone insane and that Tod had locked her up in a certain room of his home—the same eerie room in which the guests had seen the apparition of the captive woman.

The skeleton was immediately removed from its unmarked grave and, for the most part, the haunting of Tod House ended. However, back in 1950, before that discovery, *Vancouver Sun* journalists Chris Crombie and George Vipond decided to spend a night in the Tod House. They hoped to meet the ghosts and then report on their adventures. Although they saw nothing, they came away convinced that the spirits in at least one Oak Bay house were not completely at rest.

As the two tried to settle in for the night, they heard the front gate outside the house open and then close. Crombie and Vipond listened to the sounds of footsteps walking up the path toward the house. Presuming that they were about to have visitors, they prepared to answer the door. When no one knocked, the pair looked outside. No one was there.

If that incident unnerved them, it was well that the investigators did not know what surprises the night held in store for them. "There were mysterious, muffled thumps; a pitter patter that sounded like bare feet on wood; a faint but definite musical tinkle ...," they recalled.

They concluded that at the time of their stay, nearly seventy years after the original homeowner's death, at the very least Tod House still had the "strange atmosphere of a long legendary past that wraps the oak-beamed rooms in a mysterious shroud." Perhaps it might be less colourful, but more concise, to say that the Tod House was haunted.

Is Mandy Possessed?

Steve Wallace, the mayor of Quesnel in central British Columbia in the late 1990s, has not said whether he's a believer or a sceptic, but he has called a certain artifact at a local museum "a great draw for the community." Other people in the community have committed themselves more fully by asserting that the artifact is "possessed."

The controversial piece is a doll, a doll named Mandy. She is roughly 0.6 metres (2 feet) long and is estimated to be about eighty years old. She began her residency at the town's museum in 1991. Earlier that year, Lisa Sorensen of Quesnel found the toy in her grandmother's trunk. She initially intended to keep the doll for herself, but a number of unexplainable and disturbing events changed Lisa's mind. She began to hear a baby crying at night, although no baby was anywhere near. Those phantom cries were accompanied by strange and unexplainable breezes blowing inside the house. When Lisa heard a window slam closed and found the spike that was supposed to hold it open lying on the floor, she decided that she'd been associated with the doll for longer than was comfortable.

Since Mandy has been in the museum, the numbers of bizarre occurrences thought to be connected with the decidedly unattractive-looking toy have increased.

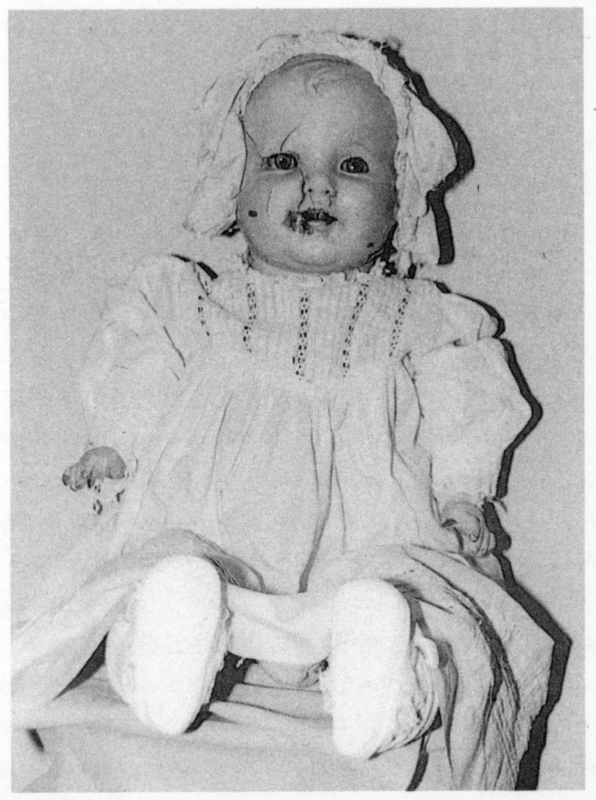

Said by many people to be possessed, Mandy has proven to be camera shy on a number of occasions.

No one has any idea who or what possesses the doll, but she has been held responsible for many eerie encounters. Some of them indicate that Mandy does not like having her picture taken. Artifacts acquired by the Quesnel and District Museum must be catalogued and photographed. While experienced museum photographer Cookie Castle was taking shots of the newly acquired doll, she and the friend who was with her during the shoot both felt extremely uncomfortable.

In order to get the job done—at least to the point where the film had been developed to produce negatives—the pair tried to ignore their feelings of discomfort. However, as soon as the negatives were hung to dry, they immediately tidied up, locked up and left the building. The next day Ruth Stubbs, the museum's curator, described the mess in the developing room as looking like "a small child had had a temper tantrum."

Ross Mitchell, a photographer with the *Cariboo Observer*, also had an interesting experience with the photos that he took at the museum. Although he photographed a number of exhibits, many of the pictures that he took were of Mandy. When Mitchell returned to his office and tried to print off contact sheets of his photographs, the paper never emerged from the developer. The potential pictures simply vanished somewhere inside the machine. While he was attempting to solve this problem, he heard footsteps in the office area above the developing room. Thinking that since he was supposedly alone in the building there must be intruders, he went up to check, but could find no source for the sounds.

Seth Gotro, a photographer with the *Quesnel Advocate*, also had a bizarre experience trying to take Mandy's picture. He reported that the doll, although it is otherwise apparently an inanimate object, seemed to "turn her head away from the lens so that I might not get her on film." Determined, nevertheless, to complete the shoot, he took the doll out of its glass case, "and sat her on the bed. She seemed to be grinning at me as the flash hit her face."

Ruth Trussler, a museum visitor from Calgary, Alberta, tried to videotape the slightly smiling doll. As she was filming, the woman remembered thinking that the doll did not like having her picture taken. Ruth did not have time to dwell on this rather odd thought, however, because an indicator light on the video recorder began to flash intermittently. When she moved along to the next exhibit, the camera worked properly again.

Mandy apparently wasn't content with disrupting the woman's filming, though. When Ruth got home and tried to play the videotape, it became wedged in her VCR and could only be removed forcibly. She never did get to view the tape that she had tried to make at the Quesnel Museum.

Perhaps one day Mandy will share her secrets with the living. Until then, those who believe that this intriguing artifact hosts a presence will have to be content with their speculations.

The Fairacres Phantom

The year was 1909, and western Canada, especially British Columbia's Lower Mainland, was enjoying a burgeoning economy. New York businessman Henry Ceperley and his bride, Grace, had recently moved to the community of Burnaby, now a city within the Greater Vancouver metropolitan area. He was a flamboyant character, but she preferred the quiet life. For ten years, until her death in 1919, Grace Ceperley spent most of her time on the grounds of the beautiful property that her husband had built. "Fairacres," as the couple called their mansion, was built beside a lake that attracted the wild birds that Mrs. Ceperley so loved. In addition, the beautiful gardens around the home were her pride and joy.

The Ceperleys' friends, as well as those in the surrounding community, probably presumed, if they even thought about it, that the couple's wealth had all come from Henry Ceperley's businesses. At best, that presumption proved to be only half true, for Mrs. Ceperley's will revealed that she was the sole owner of the house. Even more surprising than that fact was her request for its disposal. Rather than bequeathing the estate to her husband, Grace Ceperley requested that the place be sold and that the proceeds be used to construct a children's playground in Vancouver's Stanley Park. Henry Ceperley delayed in complying with his wife's request. Whether or not he ever suffered any punishment for this delay is not known. Apparently, though, Fairacres' subsequent residents paid a price for Ceperley's selfishness and disrespect.

As with the Dunsmuir residences on Vancouver Island (see "Victoria Secrets" on p. 119), Fairacres became a real-estate white elephant. It was so large and grand that even the richest folks would be hard pressed to maintain such an enormous home. Like Craigdarroch Castle—Robert and Joan Dunsmuir's greatest single monument to their wealth—the Ceperley's former home eventually became a hospital, a place that housed great suffering. The mansion also temporarily reverted to a private residence before becoming home to a mainstream religious order and then, in the late 1950s, a bizarre cult.

Much of the grand beauty that Grace Ceperley had been so proud of in her home had been destroyed by these subsequent occupants. Next, the once-dignified Fairacres became a residence for students at the new Simon Fraser University. Unfortunately, the students did not have a great deal of respect for the mansion and so its incarnation as a student residence left it badly damaged.

Just when there didn't seem to be anything more in the way of indignity that the old place could suffer, it was rescued, purchased by the Municipality of Burnaby (now a city). After considerable restoration effort and expense, the Burnaby Art Gallery (BAG) opened at Fairacres in 1967. The first reports of a ghost were not far behind.

A night-time security guard told of seeing a female apparition wearing a long, white, flowing dress that was clearly from another era. If the old-fashioned clothing had not given him a clue that he was witnessing something most unusual, the image's slight transparency certainly must have. He watched in fascination as the spirit made her way down the stairs from the third floor.

Many other employees from that early era of the BAG initially reported seeing a misty figure but, when pressed by the media, decided that they were not willing to talk about it. Some people have been more forthcoming, though. Maria Guerrero, for instance, reported that she was stunned to learn that the building's third floor was unoccupied, for she had distinctly heard noises, which had indicated to her that there was someone living up there.

Another employee, Carol Defina, also heard the ghost—or rather the swishing of the ghost's skirts. The woman made an effort not to look in the direction from which the sounds came and left the building immediately. Often, when such phantom noises have been heard, the people hearing them searched the building for intruders, but found none.

Henry Ceperley may have come back to apologize for his wrongdoing for the ghost of a man has also been seen in the art gallery. He too has been heard walking about and has been seen at the top of a staircase. It is presumed that this ghost is the one responsible for moving tools around and playing with the locks. Not surprisingly, when these sounds and movements occurred, the air pressure and temperature in the room changed.

The most recent reports from the gallery seem to indicate that the ghostly activity has abated. Perhaps the energy that manifested those restless spirits has now dissipated.

Mysterious Manifestations

Appropriately, the Maritime Museum, situated in Victoria's very haunted Bastion Square, is thought to be haunted. Anyone interested in West Coast history, marine history or ghosts will enjoy their visit here. The building was erected in 1889, replacing the courthouse and jail building that had served Victoria on that site since 1860.

The collections in the museum are so effectively compiled and displayed that even the casual visitor comes to appreciate the significance of the sea to British Columbia's heritage. A ghost-hunter should definitely not miss a trip to the top floor of the building. Getting there will, no doubt, be half the fun for, regardless of whether you take the old open-cage elevator or the staircase, you might encounter at least one of the ghostly presences in the museum.

A restored courtroom depicting the building's early days takes up most of the third floor area. This is where Chief Justice Sir Matthew Baillie Begbie held court. Begbie was widely known and just as widely feared. He earned his nickname, "the Hanging Judge," through his propensity for settling legal matters in a very permanent way. Legend has it that he once became so annoyed with a particular jury that he threatened to hang all the jurors!

Even today, upon stepping inside this re-created hall of justice, a visitor immediately senses that Begbie's presence has not left the place. A few years ago, however, two men had a much more direct encounter with the judge's spirit while they were alone in the securely locked building.

The first man, let's call him "Tom," was a technician with the museum. This particular evening, he had brought a friend, "Dick," to help him and to keep him company while he finished some chores in a third-floor workroom. As the pair finished up for the night, Tom suggested that his friend head downstairs while he tidied up and locked the room that they'd been using.

Dick agreed and started down the staircase. Because the museum was closed, all of the rooms off each landing were locked. As he was approaching the main floor, Dick could hear his friend locking up the room that they'd been working in and then starting down the stairs. Dick was completely surprised, therefore, to feel someone heading *up* the stairs, and brush past him. He whirled around quickly enough to clearly catch sight of a tall, bearded man dressed in black mounting the stairs. Too shocked to speak, Dick stood in amazement watching and listening as the figure made its way, one step at a time, up the staircase.

When Tom joined him on the main floor, Dick immediately inquired as to who the stranger had been. The technician had no idea who or what his friend was referring to—no one had passed him on the stairs. This situation was extraordinarily puzzling, because they both realized that there was nowhere that anyone could have gone to, given that every room in the building was locked. The manifestation had apparently simply dissolved before reaching Tom.

Although they probably realized (even at the time) that the image on the stairs had been a ghost, they decided that they should do the responsible thing and thoroughly search the building for possible intruders. There were none. The place was as empty and secure as they had presumed it was. The figure that Dick had seen so clearly fits the description of Sir Matthew Baillie Begbie, the Hanging Judge, who died in 1894.

Begbie probably has as much paranormal company as he could want, for Bastion Square is said to be full of spirits. In keeping with the practice of the day, public executions took place right outside that original jail and courthouse. The necessary burials that followed such hangings were more strongly influenced by expediency than respect. As a result, the executed person's remains were often simply interred under nearby paving stones. No wonder people report numerous incidents of ghostly activity.

One apparition that is seen over and over again is known as "the White Lady." She appears, seemingly out of nowhere, by the Maritime Museum. She looks quite real until those observing her presence note that she is not walking on the sidewalk but just above it. People who have followed her report that she crosses the street and then vaporizes before their eyes. Many people believe that the vision is the ghost of a local tavern owner's wife, who died in 1861.

Apparently the ghost of the harsh Judge Begbie is not content with haunting just the old courthouse, because he is also thought to have haunted a house constructed on a piece of land that he once owned in nearby Saanich, just north of Victoria. Although Begbie never lived there, it was said that he was very fond of the land and that he enjoyed visiting it. He was known to spend hours sitting on a particular boulder as he meditated. Sometime after his death, the property was sold and the new owners erected a small bungalow there. By the 1950s, that same house was deemed by mediums to be so haunted that it was, in their words, "unlivable."

There were phantom noises and plagues of pests, such as rodents and insects. An oily, silver-coloured substance of unknown origin began appearing in the basement. The haunting was so strong that it resisted all attempts at exorcism. When the letter "M" was mysteriously found scratched into a mirror, those involved with the case wondered if the scratching was possibly the ghost of Matthew Begbie making his identity known. A sequence of photographs taken on the property seemed to answer that query. When a roll of film shot at the house was developed, all the pictures turned out clearly—all except one small section of each picture, that is. As well, a misty column could be seen around the boulder on which the Hanging Judge liked to rest. The haze in the photo is dense enough to obscure all the features behind it. That mist was not visible to the naked eye at the time that the pictures were taken.

The photo frame that caused the most concern, though, showed an image of an elderly, bearded man, readily recognizable as Sir Matthew Begbie. All those who had been present attest that there had not been a person meeting that description anywhere near the property when the picture was taken.

It would be difficult to find more convincing proof that the old man had not yet left this world completely. Perhaps by now, however, his spirit has moved from the earthly realm to one where hangings are never needed.

Chapter 4

SEA LORE

The sea—so deep, so mysterious. We're drawn to it and yet, if we don't respect its power (and sometimes even when we do), it can kill us. That caveat certainly applies to the Pacific Ocean, which is often stormy, despite its name. As you might expect, ghostly legends from the sea are plentiful up and down the coast of British Columbia.

For example, a gaggle of ghosts is said to congregate each spring on the shore of Oak Bay. On a wilder part of the coast, many hikers on Vancouver Island's West Coast Trail have reported hearing the phantom cries and songs of those whose lives have been lost at sea.

There are not as many instances of ocean-going tragedies on the Pacific Ocean as there are on the Atlantic but, even so, the coast off British Columbia is not free of shipwrecks, nor free of the ghosts that inevitably seem to result from maritime disasters.

Some of those dramas are being replayed, in phantom form, even today.

The Story of the *Sea King*

One of British Columbia's most bizarre sea-tales began in San Francisco, just after the earthquake in the spring of 1906. The damage caused by the quake and the resulting fires was so severe that no one has ever been able to come up with an accurate count of those killed that spring.

During the rebuilding process, tonnes and tonnes of twisted and broken materials were hauled to the shipyards and stockpiled. It was intended that the captains of any ships dropping cargo off at the San Francisco Bay harbour could take as much of the detritus as ballast as was necessary in order to rebalance their vessels before heading out for the next port scheduled on their journey.

The *Sea King* was just such a ship. She delivered a load of wood to be used in San Francisco's reconstruction and took on an equal amount of the ballast set aside for that purpose. From her stop in San Francisco, the *Sea King* steamed north to a British Columbia port where the ballast was unloaded in preparation for the next load of cargo.

As the dock workers shovelled the ship's hold out, they were horrified to find bones mixed in among the rubble that had been used to weigh down the *Sea King*. Many of the bodies of the quake's victims had simply disintegrated or become inextricably tangled in with the debris that had been supplied as ballast.

Those who work on or next to the sea tend to be a superstitious lot at best, so finding human remains from the earthquake scattered throughout the rubble in the hold was more than enough to push most of these men over the edge. Even though there had been no untoward happenings during the voyage from San Francisco, word soon spread that the ship was cursed. As soon as she left port, the sailors swore that they could hear groans and other unexplained noises coming from the hold area.

Despite this status as an apparently haunted ship, the *Sea King* made many more uneventful voyages before being retired to the bone yard.

A Fiery Phantom

The following story is extremely well documented and equally well investigated yet, in the end, even naval authorities had to admit that they had no solution to the mystery. Retrospective assessment seems to indicate that what really occurred was simply a most unusual ghost ship sighting.

Early in November 1957, a Japanese freighter, the *Meitetsu Maru*, steamed south, past Vancouver Island, toward Seattle. The journey had been uneventful until a deckhand spotted a vessel in extreme distress. It appeared to be a fishing boat entirely engulfed in flames. The captain of the freighter ordered his craft to approach the burning vessel. As the larger craft made her way alongside, the sailors noted a strange white light just above the smaller craft. Stranger still, the light then sped away and disappeared over the horizon. Nevertheless, the *Meitetsu Maru* launched a rescue boat to assist anyone who might be stranded on the flaming fishing boat.

The Japanese delegation determined that the burning boat had already been abandoned and so simply took note of as many identifying marks on the doomed craft as possible. The sailors reported back to their captain that the boat was roughly 30 metres (100 feet) in length and that the portion of its registry number that was still visible indicated that it was a Canadian boat. They estimated that such a vessel would have required a crew of no fewer than ten to operate her.

The captain of the *Meitetsu Maru* reported his sighting to the authorities, who were not completely surprised. Several sailors had already told of seeing a bright light of unknown origin in the area at that time. Perhaps, the officials reasoned, the witnesses had spotted the glow from the burning boat.

The officials next had to determine which boat it was that had been destroyed by flames. Oddly, there were no Canadian vessels unaccounted for. Despite this fact, ships from both the United States and Canada organized an intensive search. For five days, the vessels combed more than 30,000 square kilometres (12,000 square miles) of calm ocean in good weather. They found nothing. No sign of any burnt or burning boat, or of any survivors.

An official with the American Coast Guard was so confident of the quality of the search that he stated unequivocally, "If anything had been there to find, we'd have found it."

To this day, the mystery of the flaming ghost ship off Vancouver Island has still not been solved.

The Ghostly Fate of the *Valencia*

A ghost ship or phantom ship is one of the oldest, and eeriest, of all paranormal phenomena. Sailors have reported seeing specific vessels, even hearing the officers on board bark orders at the crew, only to discover that the particular ship that they've identified sank some time before. Some sightings happen over and over again in a specific spot. Others are seen once and then never again. Such sightings are reported from all around the world, including the North Pacific in the vicinity of British Columbia.

Like the tale of the *Sea King*, the ghost story of the *Valencia* also began in 1906, as the passenger ship left San Francisco destined for Seattle. The *Valencia*, however, never made it to Seattle but ran aground on a submerged reef at Pachena Point, "the Graveyard of the Pacific," just up-island from the entrance to Juan de Fuca Strait, which she would have had to traverse on her way to Puget Sound and her destination. The ship's captain, an experienced seaman named Johnson, ordered the engines reversed at full power.

The ship shuddered mightily and then began inching backward. However, she had been badly damaged by the grounding and she rapidly began filling with water. Johnson knew that there was no point in trying to save the ship's hull at this point. It could never be repaired, so he turned his efforts to saving the lives of his passengers and crew. His only hope now, he believed, was full speed ahead in the hopes of beaching the *Valencia* and disembarking all on board.

Captain Johnson's plan might have worked at a different location, but all that he succeeded in doing here was to lodge his ship at a completely inaccessible site. He signalled for help from nearby ships but, because of the tides and rocks, none was able to get close enough to help the struggling people. The crews of rescue ships had to sit nearby, helplessly watching the dreadful plight of those trapped on board the *Valencia*. In the end, only thirty-seven souls managed to escape the shipwreck alive.

Eventually, the ship *City of Topeka* was able to approach what was left of the *Valencia* and begin the gruesome salvage process. The first job was to get the bodies off the stranded ship. After this duty was attended to and everything of value had been removed from the *Valencia*, the *Topeka* headed away from the wreck. All on board were sombre and knew that their responsibilities included informing others on the sea of the tragedy.

When they saw the first ship approach, they slowed in order to communicate the terrible news. As the vessel got closer, those on deck were stunned. The approaching ship was the *Valencia* herself or, more correctly, her ghost. The two ships sailed away from one another, the *City of Topeka* to her earthly duties, the *Valencia* to her unearthly ones.

That sighting of the *Valencia's* ghost was only the first. Sailors on board ocean-going liners occasionally spotted a wreck on the rocks near where the *Valencia* went down. The sight haunted anyone who witnessed it, for they could clearly make out the passengers and crew clinging to the riggings as their doomed vessel was battered mercilessly by the ocean's raging waves.

A ship in the distance on the high seas. It looks "real," but who knows for sure its destination, its cargo, the nature of its crew?

In addition, people who fish in the area have reported seeing spectral lifeboats manned by skeletons rowing into eternity near the site of the tragedy. As there have been no recent reports of sightings, we can hope that all those who met such a tragic end on board the ill-fated *Valencia* have now gone to their eternal rest.

Warrior's Apparition Remains

Located between North and South Pender islands in the Southern Gulf Islands, Bedwell Harbour is one of the world's most perfect natural harbours. It is not only protected from storms, but it is near plentiful springs of fresh water for sailors to enjoy and with which to replenish their ship's stores.

There is, however, one small part of the area that is best avoided, for it is haunted. The image of a tall Native warrior has been seen floating above the rocky promontory just to the north of the resort marina on the east side of the harbour. It is believed that his spirit has been there, at the site of a gruesome and tragic battle, for more than two hundred years.

The Lady in White

A ghost known as "the Lady in White" haunts a rocky shore near the Old Island Highway in the View Royal area just west of Victoria on southern Vancouver Island. The Lady's beloved husband was a sea captain during the 1800s, when shipping was far more dangerous than it is today. While he was away at sea, she often went to stay with her friends, the Calverts, at Four Mile House, their new inn in View Royal.

She died alone and lonely, before her husband returned from one of those many trips, and it is said that her watchful spirit is still not at rest. A stained-glass likeness of the Lady in White still hangs in the Calverts' former home, a tribute to the poor soul's long and fruitless vigil. (The spirits at this inn are described in "The Haunting of Four Mile House" on p. 104.)

A forlorn ghost haunts the rocky shore in this area, waiting for her love to return to her.

A Ghostly Rescue

When she was new, the *Eliza Anderson* was as fine a ship as you'd have found on the West Coast of North America. But, by 1897, the side-wheeler had served on the Olympia-Victoria mail run for nearly forty years and she was effectively worn out. Her owners, the Northwestern Steamship Company, floated the aging craft to a holding dock until they could arrange to tow her to the scrapyard. Northwestern Steamship must not have needed the money that they would recover from salvaging the *Eliza Anderson*, because the abandoned ship was left to rot in a muddy, weed-infested slough. Over the two years that she sat there, deteriorating quickly enough through natural causes, her demise was hurried along by vandals and scavengers who stripped many parts from the once-proud craft.

In August 1897, the ship was brought out of retirement for one last voyage—one destined to sail the *Eliza Anderson* into a paranormal adventure. Her crew for this trip from Victoria to Alaska via the Inside Passage was a mismatched bunch of sailors, chosen in great haste and led by a captain named Tom Powers. Potential profit was the only motive for this reclamation and so only minimal repair work was done to make the neglected and abused ship seaworthy once more.

In order to make the venture more financially rewarding, the ship's owners took on not just freight, but also passengers. Most of them were prospectors, fortune hunters much more interested in finding the golden mother-lode than in getting along with their fellow passengers. The *Eliza Anderson* was not long out of port when serious squabbles began on board. The crew members were fighting among themselves, as were the passengers. Before long, animosity developed between the two groups as well. The trip was apparently not destined to be a pleasant one.

Not long after this vessel of discontent passed the port of Prince Rupert *en route* to Alaska, she ran into a heavy storm. Tempers on board flared even further. It was not until the chief engineer came topside and reported that coal supplies were dangerously low that all of those on board the *Eliza Anderson* realized that this was no time for petty quarrels. If they didn't work together to get this ship of fools safely through the storm, none of them might be alive to tell of it.

Captain Powers immediately ordered passengers and crew alike to begin breaking apart anything on board that was flammable and not structurally necessary. If they didn't have coal, then they'd use whatever they could to generate enough steam to get them through this gale. Once a supply of flammable material was stockpiled, the majority of the badly frightened men resorted to the only other helpful activity that they could think of—prayer.

It would take divine intervention, they were sure, to keep this badly neglected, forty-year-old potential piece of scrap metal from sinking. She was being buffeted badly enough by the high waves to frighten everyone on board. When the force of the storm toppled the smokestack and sent it crashing onto the deck, all on board knew that the storm was stronger than their ship. Those who'd been to sea before knew that such an imbalance was a recipe for disaster.

Captain Powers recruited every person in his care to work toward getting the ship through the storm. He ordered some to clean the steam pumps, some to dump oil from their cargo hold onto the waves with the hope of calming them and others to work with the rudder. Those not otherwise occupied broke up more wood to stoke the fire.

Despite everyone's efforts, the best that the *Eliza Anderson* could manage was to survive standing still as the storm raged around them. The crew had no hope of generating enough power to move away from the weather. All they could do was pray that they would still be floating by the time the storm had either dissipated or moved on. After two days and two nights of constantly battling the elements, all on board were exhausted. The storm continued to rage around them. No relief appeared to be in sight. The end, in the form of certain death for all, seemed to be imminent.

By the third morning, Captain Powers had lost his bearings. He had no idea which direction was where. The situation was utterly hopeless. There was no way of knowing whether they were going to be buffeted against rocks or how much more of a beating the ship's structure would take from the winds and the waves before she started to crack. Powers knew that moments after either of those possibilities occurred, it would only be a matter of time before crew and passengers alike were all tossed to a sure death in a watery grave.

Just as their fate seemed inevitable, a sailor on the bridge thought he spotted something through the curtain of torrential rain. He hesitated before announcing his sighting, for he couldn't believe what he was seeing. There appeared to be a small boat approaching on the waves. As it came closer and closer, the sailor was able to make out an outline, an outline of a lone occupant in a woefully inadequate craft, rowing with all his might toward the *Eliza Anderson.* He tied his rowboat to the larger ship's ropes and, seconds later, "a veritable giant of a man, rawboned and muscular," was on board the distressed ship.

Captain Powers, his crew and passengers watched in disbelief as this larger-than-life figure took the wheel of their ravaged vessel. Almost imperceptibly at first, and then more obviously, the seemingly doomed ship began moving in a specific direction. No longer was she just being tossed about at the whim of the angry wind. Within hours, they'd navigated to the edge of the storm. The seas calmed and the danger lessened. Several hours later, land was in sight. The terrified souls on board the *Eliza Anderson* were no longer in peril.

As silently as he had boarded the ship, the mysterious stranger left. He made his way down a rope ladder to his little craft, untied it and rowed away. The thoughts of those left behind on the *Eliza Anderson* immediately turned from the presence who'd steered them to safety to the task of finding help in this isolated location.

It was, therefore, some time before anyone who'd experienced the unexpected rescue was ready to discuss it. By then, many of the people who had been on the ship had decided that the phantom who'd piloted them to safety had only been a figment of their collective imaginations.

In 1899, an anonymous writer, who had been on board the *Eliza Anderson* and had witnessed the supernatural rescue, submitted an article to a newspaper in Seattle. He maintained that he had recognized the saviour as the ghost of Captain Tom Wright, who had owned and operated the threatened vessel until his death. He wrote, "Captain Tom's spirit saw our danger. He knew and loved the *Anderson*, and that was how it happened that a stranger came out of the storm and brought us safely to land."

We can never know for sure what happened that stormy, fateful day off the coast of British Columbia. We only know that all on board escaped with their lives and that, having made it to Alaska, the *Eliza Anderson* never sailed again.

Chapter 5

STAGE FRIGHT

Actors, and the crews that support their theatrical efforts, tend to be a devoted, dedicated and emotional group of individuals. (They're also highly superstitious, but that's another, equally interesting story.)

The actor's job is an odd one at best: In a highly contrived setting, with the help of the crew, he or she works to convince another group of individuals, the audience, that something fictional is actually fact. Judging by the number of haunted theatres, this kind of situation is apparently a formula for phantoms.

Sagebrush Shades

They call him "Albert," "Albert the Apparition." And his presence in the Sagebrush Theatre in the south-central British Columbia city of Kamloops has been well documented over the years.

The hauntings began in 1939, just after several graves in the Lorne Street Cemetery were excavated and the bodies moved to a location on Pleasant Street, near the Sagebrush Theatre. Ever since that disruption, the image of a man has been seen frequently. It is presumed to be the spirit of Albert Mallot, the first man ever to be hanged in Kamloops.

One of Albert's favourite haunts is along the catwalk, high above the stage. Theatre technicians, people trained to be both observant and analytical, have stared in amazement at a man dressed in old-fashioned clothes who casually stands on the suspended platform. The first time that he was spotted, the worker instigated a search for what she presumed to be a trespasser. Although no one could have left that isolated area without her knowledge, she was not able to find the man. He had vanished.

The next time Albert was seen in approximately the same part of the theatre, the spectre didn't wait to be hunted down. He disappeared before the man's eyes.

After the resident phantom was seen sitting in one of the auditorium seats, employee Roger Lantz made a bold overture. He went into the seating area of the theatre and sat down in that very same spot. As soon as he was comfortably settled, Lantz challenged Albert to do something about his live presence in the ghost's preferred chair. Perhaps Roger wouldn't have been so daring if he'd known that in life Albert Mallot had a reputation for being a mean so-and-so at the best of times—and that he had been executed for having committed a cold-blooded murder. Oddly, the ghost apparently backed down from that particular challenge by Roger.

However, judging from the ghostly occurrences during the theatre performance later that night, death had perhaps only slightly improved Albert's disposition. No matter what Roger did that evening, he could not get the sound system to cooperate. The levels would not stay set. Sometimes sound would come from the wrong speaker, and sometimes not at all, with the result that cues were missed throughout the entire production. By the end of the evening, Albert had made his point to the daring Roger Lantz, who will likely never challenge a spectre again.

Though it's easy to see that Albert had an issue to settle with Roger, the ghost's instant dislike for another man, a stagehand, is more difficult to explain. Albert's motivation may have been obscure, but his sentiments were certainly made clear to the worker, who was at the time positioned on a platform high above the stage. As the worker concentrated on the job at hand, a bag of peanuts flew at him, narrowly missing hitting his head. Not only was there no human being in the area who might have propelled the missile, but to do such a thing would have been a flagrant disregard for the well-known rules of theatre safety. No one associated with the theatre would ever have done anything so disrespectful or dangerous.

Conversely, Albert's spirit has also been credited with preventing what could have been a serious accident. A woman, new to the job of operating the theatre's spotlights, came into work early one evening. She was up on the catwalk, practising lighting changes that would be required of her that night, when a voice chastised her for not wearing the requisite safety harness. Feeling embarrassed at having been found doing something so foolish, she immediately fastened the belt around herself.

Seconds later, a light crashed down from above her. Had she not been tied in, the woman would doubtless have met with a terrible accident. Badly shaken, she made her way down to the stage, wanting to thank the person who'd given her the timely warning. There was no one else anywhere in the theatre.

Albert has even been known to leave his own particular kind of ghostly "gift." An object that appears out of nowhere and for which there is no rational explanation—a sort of souvenir from an entity—is called an "apport." The appearance of an apport is a sure sign that there is a spirit around. The apports at the Sagebrush have even been heard as they materialized. When curious staff members went to check on the source of a *ping*ing sound that they heard in the backstage area, they found hundreds of tiny pebbles. Despite their efforts to solve the riddle of the mysterious appearance of these little stones, no one has ever been able to come up with a logical explanation.

Usually Albert's attempts to make his presence known are more subtle, but some employees, sensitive to the feeling of being watched by invisible eyes, have actually resigned their positions rather than endure the supernatural encounters. A cleaner, who initially announced that she was a sceptic by nature, fled the theatre after the cord of the vacuum cleaner that she was using continually became unplugged and got tied in knots. Such performances have managed to earn the ghost of Albert Mallot an accepted place in the Kamloops theatre community.

The Projectionist's Presence

Southeast of Kamloops, in Vernon, there is another haunted theatre. The Towne Theatre seems to be the permanent home of a long-dead projectionist with a bent for security.

On a number of occasions, the ghost has been heard climbing the stairs to the projection booth. Employees in the otherwise quiet theatre could then hear keys jingling before the footsteps continued across the floor of the projection room. Sometimes employee have been in the projection room when the ghost has come to "work." The people in the room at the time have reported feeling the floorboards shift as the invisible presence walked along.

An employee came in to work earlier than usual one day and, when he was satisfied that everything was ready for the evening's shows, he decided to leave for a while. Since he did not bother to lock the building's doors, he was most surprised on his return to find that they were now bolted securely. He might have attributed this mischief to a prankster, but the only way to lock the doors was with a key, and he had the only key to the doors.

In the early 1990s, a contracting company was hired to clean each of the five hundred seats in the auditorium. The workers carried their cleaning supplies into the theatre and left them on a corner of the stage. Seconds later, although no one had been near the supplies, they had moved across the stage.

The projectionist's ghost may have enjoyed having his favourite theatre cleaned, though, because he put on quite a show for the cleaners. Much to their surprise, they were entertained with music as they laboured away—phantom music, because the sound system had been turned off.

Employees at the Towne Theatre emphasize that it is an old building and old buildings can be eerie—especially when they are haunted by such an active presence.

Granville Street's Haunted Stage

In Vancouver, the Vogue Theatre on Granville Street is a striking example of art deco styling. It is also extremely haunted. Ghostly activities became noticeable in 1991, when the theatre reopened after many years of steady decline followed by total abandonment.

Perhaps it is true that ghosts like empty buildings, for the amount of paranormal activity displayed after it had been boarded up for four years was quite incredible.

One night, following a full day's work, which included stacking advertising posters in a storage room, the staff carefully locked the building as they left. The next morning, they unlocked those same bolts and discovered that the posters had been moved from the shelf that they'd been placed on and spread about the floor. This ghostly mischief sensitized the employees to their theatre's permanent inhabitants. They weren't completely surprised, therefore, to later hear unexplainable noises throughout the building.

Even knowing that they worked in a haunted building didn't help them to accept heavy fire doors opening and closing, apparently of their own free will. Those doors are located in the basement, where the theatre's former technical director Ken St. Pierre felt an invisible presence brush past him in a corridor.

Technician David Raun had a similar encounter under even more disconcerting circumstances. It was summer and brutally hot where he worked on a platform high above the stage. Anxious to get down from his perch, Raun was concentrating only on the job at hand. He was understandably startled when he felt someone brush by him. Just at that moment, the air temperature surrounding him dropped dramatically. Raun immediately looked up but, if the presence had ever been visible, it had already vanished.

Operations manager Bill Allman suffered that dreadfully uncomfortable sensation that someone was in the room with him even though he knew that he was alone. He swung around to see who'd joined him and saw only a misty shape by the door. On another occasion, Allman heard drums being played. He peered around the corner at the stage where the drums were set up, but there was no one there. Although there was one other person in the building at the time, that person was in an office well away from the stage. That night, workers who were securing the building for the night also heard the drums being played. Like Allman, they checked and found no percussionist.

Seeing an apparently solid, lifelike apparition standing stage left in the Vogue during a November 1995 show didn't cause veteran performer Shane McPherson to lose his concentration. When the image faded into invisibility before his eyes, however, McPherson was so thrown that he had to cut his dance number short.

Later in the day, McPherson questioned everyone who'd been working in the theatre during the performance. No one would admit to having seen anything out of the ordinary. The following day, after the performers had taken their last bows and the audience had left the building, technician David Raun, who'd previously only felt the ghost, walked on-stage and looked up at the projection booth. He was surprised to see someone standing there. He was even more surprised when the entity dissolved as he stared at it. When Raun and McPherson compared details about the visions that they'd been witness to, it was clear that they'd both seen the same image.

No one knows who the ghost may have been when he was alive, but he clearly has an affinity for the Vogue Theatre.

Victoria's Haunted Playhouse

Across the strait from Vancouver, in the capital city of Victoria, there are at least three haunted theatres. The Royal Theatre (see p. 100) has its supernatural goings-on and the Langham Court Theatre has its "Lady in the Loft" in residence. Then there's the McPherson Playhouse at Centennial Square, which has been home to phantoms for many years. One of those, a male ghost, can be easily explained, since the theatre has been the site of two violent deaths. In the 1920s, a theatre manager hanged himself from the balcony railing and, during the Great Depression, a gambler was murdered just outside the building. Although it is unclear exactly which man's spirit is the active one, it is presumed that one of those two tragedies is responsible for the male spectre in the theatre.

Accounting for the female apparition is a little more difficult. She's such a delightful theatre presence, though, that where she came from really doesn't matter. Because of the colour of her period dress, those associated with the theatre call her "the Lady in Grey." She is frequently seen floating about the theatre, just above the level of the floor. Occasionally she'll perch high up on the tracks that hold the stage lights. Seconds after she's been spotted, this benign entity simply fades away.

During a particularly difficult production, the ghostly lady did interfere, but perhaps unintentionally. Fittingly, the play on that occasion was about a ghost. Everyone involved agreed that no one should be invited to see the final rehearsal. They wanted the auditorium to be empty of distractions while they went through their roles one last time before the public would see—and hopefully appreciate—them. The Lady in Grey, however, disregarded the cast's wishes—or maybe she just didn't know of their needs. In any case, she walked all around the balcony area while the performers were on stage, and at one point she even ran.

The male ghost in the McPherson is much more intrusive. He's often heard walking heavily across the stage while the cast and crew meet in the basement of the otherwise empty theatre. Even though they are heard so frequently, the footsteps are so real and so loud that the people in this haunted theatre inevitably presume that someone's broken in and they set out to find the trespasser. No one is ever tracked down, nor is there ever any sign that anyone has either come into or left the locked building.

In the mid-1990s, Mary Cavanagh was working as stage manager for a production. She was "calling the show" (giving stage directions) from a seat in the cordoned-off balcony. Through the use of an earpiece and a tiny microphone, she was in voice contact with people near the stage at the time.

Although she was concentrating on the job at hand, she suddenly realized that she was not alone. There, two rows behind her, sat a formally dressed, pleasant-looking man. Mary called down to the crew below and asked that someone join her immediately. As she waited for her help to arrive, she stared in disbelief at the smiling figure. When the man whom she'd summoned opened the balcony door, the entity instantly vanished.

Given some of the ghostly antics that have been witnessed at the playhouse over the years, it's reasonable to believe that there are more than just two spectres haunting the building. A night-time security guard once heard someone walking on the fly gallery, high above the stage. As the startled man heard the footfalls coming from a place that he knew to be unoccupied, he watched as a single rope in a group of ropes (running from the floor of the stage up to the flies above) spun madly. This incident was possibly the work of a former stagehand's spirit.

The same security guard also experienced one of the most fascinating ghostly episodes ever to have occurred in the McPherson, this one an auditory one. While on his rounds, he heard party sounds coming from the green-room, which is a place for actors to await their on-stage time. Many theatres have a tradition of post-production meetings that take place in the green-room. Cast and crew members attending these debriefing sessions can be quite expressive, and the meeting can become quite loud.

However, all this racket was occurring in the wee hours of the night, when the guard was supposedly alone in the building. Upon investigation, he found an empty room. Presumably he had heard just the ghostly residue of such a gathering. Understandably, the man was not anxious to work another night shift.

Royally Haunted

The McPherson Playhouse is administratively associated with Victoria's equally haunted Royal Theatre on Broughton Street. This link means that employees from one venue sometimes get asked to work at the other. As a result, at least one unsuspecting worker got the ghostly fright of his life.

A regular McPherson employee, Blair Morris, was assisting at the Royal during a busy time in 1988. He was locking up the unfamiliar venue and when he crossed the stage he suddenly felt as though someone had stabbed him in his back. When Morris reported the frightening incident to Larry Eastick, a worker more familiar with the Royal, the latter listened with the compassion borne of experience. Over the years, many people had suffered the same horrible feeling in exactly that same spot.

The regular employees had developed a routine of working in pairs, which they found helped them to avoid becoming psychic stabbing victims. This buddy system also allowed them to alleviate the usually more subtle—but also more pervasive and sometimes overwhelming—feeling that they were not welcome in the theatre after closing time.

In 1990, a night-time custodian working on the theatre's main floor happened to glance up at the balcony area. He was most surprised to see a man up there. The place was supposed to have been empty at that hour. However, since the theatre was being used as the venue for a series of televised religious services at the time, the cleaner assumed that someone involved in the production had fallen asleep in one of the seats. He immediately headed upstairs to help the man find his way out. Despite a thorough search, first of the balcony area and then the remainder of the theatre, the custodian could not find another human being in the building.

Assuming that the straggler had found his own way out, the cleaner continued with his duties. Moments later, he looked up toward the balcony for a second time. There, once again, was the man. This time the custodian ran to the balcony in order to apprehend the intruder. However, when he got there just seconds later, there was no sign of anyone, nor any sign that anyone had ever been there. The terrified worker fled the building. Since that ghostly incident, all routine cleaning at the Royal has been done during the daylight hours.

Chapter 6

THE SPIRIT'S INN

A room in a hotel, motel or an inn of any sort can serve as a home away from home for weary travellers. Therefore it shouldn't be too surprising that, like haunted houses, many of these temporary lodgings also have resident ghosts.

As the next few stories demonstrate, like ghosts anywhere, these hostelry-based spirits can range from being barely noticeable to being a terrible nuisance.

The Haunting of Four Mile House

Four Mile House, on Vancouver Island's Old Island Highway (Highway 1A) in the community of View Royal, is one of the most delightfully haunted places in the province. The building's long and colourful history has provided the establishment with both character and characters.

One of the ghosts thought to be haunting the place is the spirit of Jake Matteson, who settled in the area during the mid-1800s when Four Mile House was a popular new stopping place for folks travelling up-island in horse-drawn carriages. Matteson had apparently left the love of his life behind in Scotland while he ventured out to establish a home for them in the New World. He worked feverishly to amass the money that he needed. To protect his growing fund, he kept it hidden in the depths of a well near Four

Mile House. Unfortunately, the enterprising Scotsman died before he and his love were reunited. To this day, his stash has never been found. Perhaps the rumours about his ghost staying behind to guard the money that he worked so hard to accumulate are true.

Jake was never reunited with his lady-friend in life, but in death he might be keeping company with the soul of a woman named Margaret Gouge. She lived at Four Mile House during a period just following Jake's untimely death. Margaret loved flower gardens so much that her spirit is still seen gazing upon the gardens that surround her former home.

When Wendy and Graham Haymes purchased Four Mile House in the 1980s, the once distinguished house was badly in need of attention. They set about doing the necessary renovations and, right from the start, were aware that their restoration efforts were being watched by an unseen presence.

Ghosts are generally restless when their haunts are being renovated, but this entity, whoever he or she was, reacted quite differently. Some days, just after the flesh-and-blood folks had packed away their tools for the day, the ghost apparently took its turn, for the couple could often hear the sounds of phantom hammering and sawing. Unfortunately, if the presence ever accomplished anything, it wasn't noticed.

There's also a more recent ghost associated with the building. He's a middle-aged man, probably from around the 1940s. People report seeing him as he sits at a table, appearing to pore over paperwork. As soon as anyone approaches his image, it vanishes. After a sighting, the chair on which he had been sitting is left slightly askew—evidence that assures that his visit cannot easily be forgotten.

The story of "the Lady in White" (see p. 85) is also associated with this inn.

Haunted Restaurants

The Keg Restaurant chain is known for its fine beef. Perhaps it should also be known for its ghosts. The Keg Restaurant in the heart of Toronto is housed in a huge, old mansion—a huge, old, *very haunted* mansion (see Chapter 7 of my *Ontario Ghost Stories*). The Keg in historic New Westminster, on the north bank of the Fraser River a short distance east of Vancouver, is housed in the old train station on Columbia Street—the old train station with the haunted basement.

Most members of this restaurant's staff dislike being in the basement. Many simply refuse to go into it alone. Those who are brave enough to do so have been rewarded by hearing their names called out by a phantom voice.

About four blocks up Columbia Street from the Keg there's another place where you can count on spirits with your meal. The building that houses the Met Hotel and restaurant is one of the few in the city to predate the devastating fire that swept the area in 1886. The ghosts that inhabit the place aren't quite that old, but they've haunted the hotel long enough that they are all now thought of as being permanent residents.

At least three ghosts are in residence at The Met. "George" is the resident apparition in the restaurant. He appears to be so solid that when people first see him they are convinced that he is a real person.

After he calmly walks through a solid wall, they're understandably less convinced.

On the fourth floor there are two apparitions: a man and a woman. They are seen dressed in old-fashioned clothing, their images surrounded by a light that gives the entities a white hue. Staff at the hotel enjoy these presences because they seem to infuse the area that they're in with a peaceful feeling.

Despite the positive effect that they have on flesh-and-blood witnesses, the presences seem unaware of today's world. They simply stand near the elevator on the hotel's fourth floor, chatting away to one another.

Like the ghost in the basement of New Westminster's Keg, the ghost in the Old Spaghetti Factory in Vancouver's Gastown delights in calling out employees' names, in a voice that echoes eerily through the building.

This restaurant's unusual decore incorporates a restored old trolley car. Many people maintain that the area in and around the vehicle feels haunted, and no doubt it is. There is even a half-century-old photograph on display that shows a shadowy figure sitting in the supposedly empty trolley. Inexplicably, even today that same shadowy figure is sometimes seen sitting quietly in one of the seats.

Susie's Spirit

The town of Zeballos, between Nootka and Kyuquot sounds on the west coast of Vancouver Island, was for a while in the late 1930s a hub of great economic excitement an energy. Veins of gold had been discovered in the area and folks were coming from far and wide, hoping to tap into the valuable natural resource. Just as those who had sought gold during the rushes of the 1800s had required services, so did the would-be miners of that later era.

As people attempted to supply those services, Zeballos became something of a boom town. Businesses catering to the miners' needs cropped up as required. Those undertakings in turn brought even more people to the area.

Susie Woo was one of those who toiled away at a job created by the gold rush. She washed laundry at the town's hotel. Part of the arrangement in her employment apparently dictated that she also lived in the hotel. And history tells us that Susie eventually died there.

The circumstances of the woman's death were not suspicious, so the hotel's owners merely re-did her room and began renting it out along with all the others in the building. This approach was clearly not an idea that pleased Susie's spirit. The first encounter with the laundry worker's ghost did no more than startle the guests in Susie's former home. She simply appeared to them, but that appearance was enough to have them ask for alternative accommodation.

By the second sighting, Susie's ghost had become more aggressive, because she chased three men out of the room, down the stairs and into the lobby. If she intended to frighten them away, her tactic was effective, because they refused to go back to the room even to pick up the possessions that they'd left behind.

A man employed by the hotel to make minor repairs apparently refused to be dictated to by a phantom. The man confronted Susie's spirit and told her not to bother him. She never did again.

For the most part, though, people associated with the Zeballos Hotel are content to let Susie Woo have her eternity alongside their lives. When they hear footsteps in an empty hallway or feel that they are not alone—or, worse, are being closely watched—they know that Susie's merely making her presence felt. The hotel's owners have made one concession: the room that Susie once called home is no longer rented out to overnight guests but is used now as an office. Susie's spirit seems to appreciate this change.

An Occasional Visitor

As we all know, the "good old days" were not really as "good" as many people would like us to believe. Nostalgia and romance have a way of colouring our sentiments, no matter what the time period. On the West Coast of the nineteenth century, tragedies and violence were a constant feature of the frontier landscape. This history has created some enduring ghostlore for us to ponder.

The Heriot Bay Inn on Quadra Island, near Campbell River, was a busy spot in the 1890s. For the most part, the loggers came and went. One logger, however, didn't go far. After the man was killed in a brawl at the hotel, his body was hastily interred on an adjoining property. Many people are sure that his spirit has not yet left and occasionally roams about the inn.

In the wee hours one night in the 1980s, the auditory detritus of that fatal fight so long ago may have bubbled to the surface. A man was alone in the hotel at approximately 2 AM when he heard what he reported as "a loud racket outside." Suspicious that animals were getting into the garbage bins, he ran outside to chase them away. When he got outside, however, there was nothing to see.

Feeling puzzled, he turned to go back into the building. What he saw then gave him a worse fright than the noise that he'd just heard, for every light on the first floor of the hotel was blazing. None had been on just seconds before when he'd come out. Thinking then that an intruder had broken in, the man searched the building, but he wasn't able to find anything or anyone that might be responsible.

Another incident took place on a quiet autumn afternoon in 1987. A woman tending bar at the Heriot Bay Inn decided to take advantage of the lack of afternoon customers by stocking the fridge in anticipation of the inevitable evening gathering. As she did so, she heard someone come into the bar.

She carefully set the bottles on the shelves in the chiller before turning around completely. In her peripheral vision, however, she had clearly seen her first customer of the day—or so she presumed. It was a man, dressed in old-fashioned clothing, similar to that worn by people that she'd seen in old local photographs. When she turned to greet the man, however, she found herself staring into an empty room.

A man staying in the hotel one winter swore that he frequently heard phantom footfalls in the hallway outside his room. Whenever he checked, there was never anyone there. Once, when he and the hotel's manager were alone together in the building, they both heard the mysterious sounds. They searched the premises immediately and thoroughly, but found no one, nor any indication that anyone had been there.

As the ghost of the logger has never presented himself as menacing in any way, his presence has now been accepted as simply a quirky part of the area's history.

Atlin's Smoking Spirit

The tiny town of Atlin, nestled in the extreme northwest of British Columbia, was once home to a persistent ghost with a bad habit. For many years, this phantom resided in the room over the office of the Kootenay Hotel.

It was believed that the ghost was the impatient spirit of a former long-term guest at the hostelry who smoked heavily but could not be trusted with matches. In order to protect themselves, their building and all their guests, the hotel's proprietors instructed the woman to tap on the floor of her room whenever she wanted to smoke. Whoever was in the office below would hear the sound and go up to light her cigarette for her.

This system worked well until one occasion when the employee working the front desk was busy and thus not able to respond immediately to the familiar signal. Perhaps this time the woman wanted more than just to have her cigarette lit because, by the time the man got to her room, she had died.

The authorities were contacted and the woman's remains were removed but, oddly, the tapping sounds continued to be heard coming from the room over the office. A guest who stayed awhile in a room across the hall from the haunted one reported that he heard tapping at the same time every evening.

Staff heard the phantom's demands as well. The building was carefully examined in the hopes of revealing a logical cause for the strange noises, but no physical reason for the sounds was ever discovered.

The phantom tapping continued intermittently until November 1969, when the Kootenay Hotel burned to the ground. Perhaps the impatient guest finally got the ultimate light for that last cigarette that she never got to smoke.

Casper Hasn't Checked Out

The management and staff at a certain motel in the community of Williams Lake, approximately midway between Kamloops and Prince George, have named their ghost "Casper." Like the cartoon ghost of that name, theirs enjoys playing pranks; though he doesn't appear to mean any harm to anyone, he can make the simplest chore a challenge.

On two occasions when members of the housekeeping staff were cleaning a room in preparation for a new guest, they found that there were no hangers in the closet. They left the room just long enough to get some but, when they returned moments later, a more-than-adequate supply of hangers was in place.

Like many ghosts, Casper seems attracted to both television sets and water faucets. He'll turn both on when the living beings in a room are least expecting it. He doesn't always seek out company, though; often, when staff members are in the laundry room, they can hear his footsteps somewhere above them.

No one seems to have any idea who Casper may have been when he was alive. All they know for sure is that in death he happily haunts the motel.

The Manifestation at the Arms

Port Moody, just east of Vancouver, also has a haunted hotel. The Port Moody Arms Hotel, as it used to be called, has long been home to at least one ghost, and more recently to two distinct personalities. The first spirit has been evident since the mid-1950s. A couple in residence there for an extended period at that time frequently reported hearing the sounds of phantom footsteps in the hallway outside their room. A fire extinguisher in their room would shake rapidly when there was nothing physically present to cause the movement. This spirit's most energetic stunt, repeated often during the mid-1950s, consisted of rearranging a room that had been set up in a particular way for a forthcoming meeting.

It is the ghostly duo of "Slim and his dog," however, who have startled more than their fair share of folks at the Port Moody Arms Hotel. And that's a shame, for neither the man nor his faithful canine companion ever meant to do anyone any harm. They lived a quiet existence at the hotel in the late 1970s. In return for his keep, Slim helped to keep the place clean.

After Slim died in 1978, employees began to report definite feelings of unease in certain areas of the hotel. They were sure that they were being watched by an invisible presence, and yet no one ever indicated that they felt threatened.

As recently as 1986, Slim's apparition was seen by a woman preparing to open the cocktail lounge. She had no trouble recognizing the plaid shirt that Slim had always worn. That same year, the resident ghost was also credited with having played a record on an antique gramophone kept on the premises.

When Debbie Yurkoski, a new employee in the pub, went downstairs for supplies one time, she saw an image of a man who merely stood and watched her. Understandably, she fled. Although (as she later discovered) the apparition matched Slim's description, she'd never heard the stories about the benign ghost at the Port Moody Arms and therefore had no idea whether or not she was potentially in danger.

The most trouble that Slim and his dog ever caused can only be classed as a bit of mischief. They unlocked previously locked doors, opened closed ones, turned on appliances, and moved drinking glasses around. Staff members learned to address Slim's ghostly presence occasionally as they went about their daily chores. This tactic seems to have kept the ghost content.

And, although no one reported actually seeing or sensing the dog, Slim and his faithful four-legged friend were so close in life that everyone who knew them found it hard to believe that they weren't enjoying their eternity together.

Whose Afterlife is It, Anyway?

Custody battles are common enough these days, but this dispute is of a slightly different nature. The ghostly difference of opinion centres around the spirit of the Harbour House Hotel's former owner, Walter Herzog.

The attractive Harbour House, located in the town of Ganges on Saltspring Island, has been thought to be haunted since Herzog's murder in September 1973. In life, the man loved the place and it's really no wonder. Many people consider Ganges to be one of the most desirable places to live in all of Canada. Herzog not only enjoyed the location but had invested an enormous amount of money and energy into the hotel itself. His life may have been cut short by a burglar, but the thief could not steal Herzog's association with the hotel.

Walter Herzog, or his spirit at least, is frequently heard sweeping floors and sometimes moving furniture about. Even when he isn't making noise, people are still able to detect the ghost's presence. They encounter columns of cold air and inexplicable and sudden changes in air pressure, and they experience a distinct sensation that they are not alone in a room where they can see no one else.

In order to check this haunting out from a firsthand perspective, fellow ghost-story author Jo-Anne Christensen and I travelled to the haunted inn. As most of the ghostly activity centres around one particular room, we asked to stay in that one. Usually this room is not rented out to paying customers, but is either left empty or assigned to members of bands that have gigs at the hotel.

By morning, the musicians are often found asleep in their vans, having been driven out of their supplied accommodation by the spectral sounds of moaning, or by disembodied voices whispering not-quite-audible words.

Jo-Anne and I, though, slept undisturbed in the room where the phantom's frolics have sent many a macho young man screaming into the night. After spending such an uneventful night in the basement suite—and given that Walter is credited with turning off and even occasionally unplugging the jukebox—I suspect that Walter's unfriendly treatment of musicians is probably just because he is not a lover of today's music. Ann Ringheim, the Harbour House manager, certainly appears to support that contention in a newspaper interview in which she is quoted as saying, "We've decided he [the ghost of Walter Herzog] doesn't like bands at all."

The ghost is not above a little fun, however, for he plays the pinball machine for prolonged periods of time. He also likes to turn on water faucets, beer taps, television sets and calculators when no one is near them. Sceptics who might want to blame the electrical oddities on power surges should note that these occurrences have been observed even when the appliances are not plugged into any power source.

This bizarre state of affairs helped to prepare the staff for the problems that they had with the telephone line into one particular room. After receiving many calls from Room 206 when it was not rented out, the management decided to disconnect that phone line entirely. This precaution would no doubt have solved the problem if it hadn't been for Walter's presence. According to the lights on the main switchboard, calls continued to be initiated from Room 206, even though it was technically no longer possible. The location of that room might have had a bearing on the situation, for it is directly above the area where Walter was killed.

Despite these inconveniences, the staff are pleased to have Walter's ghostly presence with them in the hotel. Not only do they enjoy his antics, but they feel protected when he is around. They overwhelmingly want to keep their ghost at the Harbour House Hotel. This desire forms one-half of the basis for the custody battle. Conversely, Alexei Rainier, an area psychic, wants the hotel exorcised to set Herzog's spirit free.

Manager Ann Ringheim wanted to know if the hotel's ghost was happy spending his eternity at the hotel, so she asked him for a sign. Walter apparently did his best to communicate with the mortals via a series of numbers on the telephone switchboard display. Ann understood these numbers to correspond to the letters B-O-O and interpreted this response as Walter's way of indicating that he was enjoying himself. Alexei, however, interpreted the same numbers as the word "no," so the situation remained unresolved.

For better or for worse, the ghost of Walter Herzog continues to make his presence known to some of the folks at the Harbour House Hotel.

Chapter 7

CLASSICALLY HAUNTED

Some of British Columbia's ghost stories are absolute classics, staples of the genre. Because these particular tales have been around for so long, they are perhaps more correctly known as ghostly legends. Whatever label you choose to attach to the following anecdotes, they are undeniably intriguing.

Victoria Secrets

The Dunsmuir name has been firmly entrenched in British Columbia's history. Today, well over a century after the Dunsmuirs arrived, the Dunsmuir spirit lives on.

Robert and Joan Dunsmuir emigrated from Scotland in 1851 to begin their rags-to-riches tale in the Victoria area. Their first home was little more than a shack and yet, by 1887, they were the wealthiest people on Vancouver Island and construction of their thirty-nine-room castle was underway. Robert had invested heavily in coal mining and railways. Both interests paid off handsomely and he became rich, probably beyond his wildest dreams.

Along with wealth comes power, but in Robert Dunsmuir's case, it meant more than just monetary power. He also gained political power. He first became premier and, later, the lieutenant-governor of British Columbia. Considering this self-propelled meteoric rise, it is really no wonder that Dunsmuir felt that his family's residence should be nothing short of palatial. Tragically, the otherwise successful man didn't succeed in living to see his dream home become a reality. He died in 1889, while "Craigdarroch Castle," as he'd chosen to call the huge house, was still under construction.

Just months later, daughter Agnes Dunsmuir and her husband, James, also died. In the summer of 1890, Joan Dunsmuir, her three unmarried daughters, and her recently orphaned grandchildren made the long-awaited move into "the Castle."

Joan lived another eighteen years, apparently enjoying her luxurious home and her status as the reigning social queen of Victoria's high society. After her death in 1908, however, Craigdarroch Castle effectively became a white elephant on the real-estate market. It was far too large and expensive for most people to consider purchasing it as a residence. Yet, its four floors, ornate detailing, eighteen fireplaces and immense main staircase meant that it was not suitable for commercial use. As a result, the castle was renovated over and over again in order to meet many different needs, including that of hospital, school and office building. Every now and again, demolition seemed to be inevitable.

Fortunately, an energetic group of concerned Victoria citizens formed The Castle Society in 1969. Months later, they took over control of Craigdarroch and began the enormous job of returning the badly deteriorated building to its former glory.

Not long after the renovations got underway, workers began to notice some decidedly unusual qualities about the place. Although the stories of the workers' bizarre experiences are now officially denied by staff at the castle, they have been well documented over the years. During a visit to Craigdarroch in the early 1990s, a guide treated me to quite an extensive dialogue about the spirits residing in the place.

A man working on the restoration process reported one of the first ghostly encounters. While relaxing during his lunch break, the worker saw a woman's satin slipper on a disembodied foot and the hem of a ball gown. This partial apparition "walked" down a few stairs before disappearing as mysteriously as it had appeared.

Since the restoration, visitors and employees alike have had supernatural experiences in the beautiful old home. Although the spirits do not always take the form of an actual visual manifestation, they make their presences known nevertheless. The lilting strains of piano music, when there is no physical reason for such sounds, have been heard. There are even phantom smells—such as the distinct odour of candle wax, when no candles have been in use.

Sudden cold drafts shouldn't be surprising in such a big, old place, but they can occur at Craigdarroch Castle even on the warmest summer afternoon. The agony suffered by patients during the time that the Castle was a hospital is still reportedly felt by sensitive visitors. One tour guide acknowledged to me that he could detect the memories of their suffering in certain rooms. Perhaps the most puzzling presence is the apparition of a little girl who is occasionally seen in the basement.

Most of the ghosts in the Castle seem oblivious that they are no longer of this realm. Instead, they seem trapped somehow in their own time and place. The result is that though their presences may be unnerving to those of us who are alive today, they appear to mean us no harm. They simply haven't fully left Craigdarroch Castle.

One employee explained that she'd finally come to realize there were "people from the past" among those from the present. As an example, she related a couple of anecdotes. During a break in a meeting, those attending began to get up and leave the room. The noise that they made doing so must have attracted the attention of the spirit of a long-dead maid for, clad in a uniform from the Victorian era, she stepped into the room, looked all about and then disappeared.

The employee also spoke of an evening meeting when those gathered were preparing to leave. A woman in the crowd asked, "What about the man in the bowler hat?" Everyone in attendance looked blankly at the woman who'd spoken. She was pointing to a chair. To everyone else in the room, that chair appeared to be empty. The concerned guest later explained that she knew herself to be "slightly psychic."

The least surprising of the spirits is Joan Dunsmuir herself. The suite of rooms on the second floor where she spent most of her last years has a particular feel to it. Neither fellow ghost-story author Jo-Anne Christensen nor I claim to be psychic and yet, when we were touring the Castle, we both immediately detected a very different ambiance in what had been Joan's private sitting-room. There seemed to be a change, an increase, in the air pressure there. We weren't surprised, therefore, when a guide told us that there existed considerable, tangible proof that the lady of the house was still in residence.

"Once there was a display case set up in Joan's sitting-room," noted our informant. "It had a top hat and a walking-stick or umbrella or something in it. I remember that the display was fine when the castle was locked up for the night but, the next morning, both the hat and stick had been knocked off the stand inside the glass case [which was securely locked!]."

It seemed that the late Mrs. Dunsmuir did not approve of other people's possessions in *her* area of the house. Somehow that seems only fitting—proof that "the Queen" still presides over her Castle.

The Dunsmuir legacy continued, both palatially and politically, for one more generation. James Dunsmuir, Joan and Robert's older son, went on to do much of what his father had done—and more—including leaving haunted Hatley Castle in Colwood, just to the west of Victoria, as a permanent legacy. Like Craigdarroch Castle, it remains, in all its haunted splendour, accessible to the public.

Unlike his father, James Dunsmuir—along with his wife, Laura—did get to enjoy living in his expensive and expansive masterpiece. In 1907 he bought Hatley Park on Sooke Road, the first parcel of what was to eventually total over 300 hectares (about 800 acres) of land, and immediately approached architect Sam Maclure with specific and grand instructions. He added, "Money doesn't matter." By 1909, Hatley Castle was completed and, judging by the finished product that still proudly stands today, architect Maclure listened well to the man who'd contracted his services.

The estate and the roads running through it are surrounded by a most impressive stone wall. During the Dunsmuirs' residency, the grounds within that wall required a maintenance staff of one hundred workers. Hatley Castle itself, with its stone exterior, is as elegant as any you'll find in Britain or Europe. The interior finishes

Hatley Castle, built to be the luxurious home of James and Laura Dunsmuir, is said to be haunted.

include the lavish use of expensive materials, with pewter fixtures, oak and rosewood panelling and teak floors.

James Dunsmuir retired to his grand home and lived there until his death in 1920. Laura, who loved her impressive home possibly even more than her husband did, remained in residence until her death in 1937. And there are those who say that she still hasn't left.

As with Craigdarroch Castle, disposing of this expensive Dunsmuir property after the widow's death became a considerable problem. Hatley Castle sat empty, deteriorating, for three years until the federal government purchased it for use as a military college. Buying this castle and the surrounding land may have been one of the few bargains that the Canadian government has ever managed. They paid Laura Dunsmuir's estate a total of $75,000 for this piece of real estate. Coincidentally, that amount was the exact sum that Robert Dunsmuir had paid merely to erect the stone wall surrounding the property.

For the next fifty-four years, Hatley Castle served as the site of Royal Roads Military College and provided office space for additional Canadian Armed Forces personnel. Some of the cadets who trained there went home with the proverbial stories to tell their grandchildren. On the upper floors, where Laura Dunsmuir spent most of her final days, the cadets occasionally reported feeling "webs of icy thread being brushed across" their skin when they were "burning the midnight oil" in order to prepare for tests.

Others actually saw Laura's spirit. She appeared clearly enough that they were able to describe her, and therefore confirm that it was definitely the former mistress of the manor. However, they also knew that what they were seeing wasn't a corporeal being, for her image was slightly see-through.

Despite this lack of visual strength, at least one student went away convinced of the spectre's physical strength. He awoke to her tugging on his leg. When he tried to pull away, she pulled back and he had quite a struggle before he was able to yank his leg free of her ghostly grasp. When he finally did succeed in pulling his leg free, the image vanished.

Today the cadets are gone and Royal Roads Military College has become Royal Roads University, one of the most innovative public universities in Canada. It will be interesting to watch this new educational concept develop and, for ghost hunters, to see if the spirit of Laura Dunsmuir will at last release her hold on her beloved Hatley Castle.

The Gravlin Ghosts

The following British Columbia ghost story has become a Canadian classic.

When the popular Victoria *Times* sports editor Victor Gravlin married his girlfriend, a privately employed nurse named Doris, no one could have predicted that their love story would end in tragedy. As it turns out, their story would never really have an ending at all. No one alive today recalls the exact date on which the pair was married, but it is known that they had separated by 1934. Although she still cared for him, Doris could no longer tolerate what Victor's drinking was doing to both his health and their marriage. She packed her bags and moved on.

The pair maintained contact with one another, however, and so Doris did not consider it odd that Victor contacted her and asked her to go for a walk with him on September 22, 1936. They met at the Oak Bay Beach Hotel. What happened after that meeting can only be conjecture. Doris may have noticed that her husband seemed exceptionally depressed that day. Certainly, others who had dealt with him that week recall being concerned about his apparent unhappiness. All that is known for sure is that neither Doris nor Victor Gravlin was ever seen alive again.

Doris's body was found five days later when John Johnson, a caddy at the Victoria Golf Course, went looking for an errant golf ball. He probably never found that ball—moments after discovering Doris Gravlin's partially dressed and badly beaten body he called the police. The authorities immediately began to search for Victor Gravlin. Four weeks later they found him, or at least the remains of him, floating face down in Oak Bay, with Doris's shoes in his pockets. It appeared that the deceased were victims of a murder-suicide.

The tragic events were duly noted in the local papers and then for the most part forgotten—at least until the mid-1960s, when Doris's ghost began appearing. Since then, there have been dozens of manifestations of the murdered woman's soul. She always appears in the spring, prompting the moniker "the April Ghost." And there are other consistencies in all the Doris Gravlin sightings. For instance, a dark mood prevails just before she appears, and a seemingly directionless wind begins to blow, while the air becomes cold and clammy.

In 1964, two youths watched a "misty grey female shape, skim effortlessly over the rocky landscape by the water." It was clear to both of the young people that what they were witnessing was not of this realm. Others who have seen Doris, however, say that the ghost is in such a solid form that at first they presume that she is a real person. Still others report being frightened by an image clad in white running toward them and then vanishing before their eyes in a pool of white light.

Some witnesses describe seeing a woman dressed in a brown suit and looking very much alive, just impossibly out of place in her 1930s-style clothing. She stands at the side of the road, as if waiting to cross. The majority of the witnesses to that version of the apparition are convinced that they've seen a real person, not a ghost. The only point for those folks to ponder is why the lady's wearing a period costume, and one that's out of season to boot.

A filmier image of Doris is also seen wearing a white dress. Some say that it is a wedding gown that she has on, and others are inclined to think that it's her nurse's uniform that they've seen her wearing.

If it was indeed her husband who killed her, perhaps that's why Doris seems to enjoy tormenting men. George Drysdale was walking with some friends when he spotted the ghost in front of him. He immediately turned away in shock, only to find that the ghost was instantly in front of him once again. He whirled around a second time, but she persisted, effectively boxing him in, as the others in his group looked on in horrified amazement. Finally, possibly tiring of her game, Doris's apparition disappeared as quickly as it had appeared.

Victor's spirit must have gone on immediately to its final reward, because no one has ever reported either seeing or sensing it. Every spring, however, the faithful still gather to wait for the April Ghost to appear near the Victoria Golf Course at Oak Bay.

There is another interesting spin on this long-standing ghost story. Some people believe that the ghost is not Doris's at all—they maintain that she is the ghost of Victor Gravlin's mother, who walks the area looking for her deceased son. Those who believe this version of the legend generally also feel that Victor was innocent in Doris's death. As the only two who know the truth are certainly no longer alive to share it with us, we are left to make our own decisions as to the identity of the ghost and the guilt or innocence of the various parties.

Fernie Folklore

The heritage of the town of Fernie, in the Elk Valley in southeastern British Columbia, is tied to a piece of ghostly folklore.

Legend tells us that in the late 1890s, during one of his expeditions to the area, prospector William Fernie, after whom the town is named, noticed an unusual piece of jewellery around a First Nations maiden's neck. The necklace was made of shiny black stones, which he recognized as being coal—a mineral that he had been searching for. If he could find the cache that those nuggets came from, Fernie was sure that he would become very wealthy.

The would-be miner's inquiries indicated that the maiden wearing the pieces of coal was the chief's daughter. He approached the tribal leader and asked where the chunks had been found. The girl's father apparently decided that, if the white man's agenda was going to be satisfied, his would be too. The Native leader proposed that he and Fernie enter into something of a partnership. The chief would show the explorer where the coal had been mined if, in return, William Fernie would take his daughter's hand in marriage.

Fernie initially agreed to the bargain but, as soon as he learned the location of the valuable natural resource, he went back on his word.

The chief and his daughter were both angry and insulted. Not only had the white man failed to deal honourably, he had also offended them.

The Native leader responded by placing a curse on the settlement that bore the prospector's name. He decreed that fire, flood and famine would ensue. In order to be certain that even insensitive white people would never be able to forget the inexcusable wrong perpetrated by their forefather, the chief created a permanent reminder on Mount Hosmer. According to the Fernie Chamber of Commerce, "The ghost rider of Mount Hosmer can be seen each sunny summer evening on a rock face high above the city. The 'ghost' is a spectacular shadow in the form of an Indian Princess sitting on a horse with her father, the chief, walking beside her, leading the horse."

Even without such a dramatic visual reminder of the curse, it is unlikely that anyone could have doubted the effectiveness of the chief's power. The first devastating fire burned through the burgeoning community in 1904, seven years after the invective had been issued. Four years later, when Fernie had recovered from the devastation of the first fire, a forest fire spread to the town and all but destroyed it.

Next came the threatened flood. In 1916 the Elk River overflowed its banks, flooding parts of the beleaguered settlement. In the 1930s, the Great Depression, although worldwide, had such a profound effect on the Elk Valley area that many Fernie residents concluded that their suffering was a further effect of the chief's curse. The spirit of the wronged chief finally had the attention of the townsfolk, but it took a further thirty years before his spectre would be laid to rest and the curse lifted.

On August 15, 1964, at a ceremonial assembly, Kootenai Chief Ambrose Gravelle (Chief Red Eagle) invited Fernie Mayor James White to join him in smoking the peace-pipe, symbolically signifying a final resolution between the two groups and at last lifting the curse.

Although an accord now exists between the non-Natives and the Natives in the area, some versions of this ghostly legend indicate that the tale is so accepted in local lore that First Nations people will still only camp overnight in the area when there is absolutely no alternative. In this way, and through the shadowy reminder on Mount Hosmer, the ghost of the chief and his daughter remain presences in the area.

An Understandably Unsettled Soul

Craigflower School in Saanich, north of the capital city of Victoria on Vancouver Island, was destined to be haunted before it was ever built. Although no one knew it in 1855, when the first building was being constructed, the educational leaders of this burgeoning community had chosen to build, if not on top of an ancient Native burial site, then certainly right next to it. Recent archeological exploration has revealed artifacts proving that the land has been used by humans for more than 2500 years. Despite this tenure, no ghostly activity was noted until 1911, when a new school was built and the original building was relegated to serve as the caretaker's residence.

From the moment it began, however, this haunting was a dramatic and full-blown one. One evening, early on in their tenancy at the residence, Mr. & Mrs. Hugh Palliser were relaxing in their kitchen when they heard the door of the adjacent woodshed open. Hugh Palliser got up to welcome whoever their unexpected guest might be and show him or her in via the proper door. However, the house door opened before he had a chance to get to it—but all that came in was a rush of dreadfully cold air, even though it was a calm September evening and that it was quite warm outside.

A quick investigation failed to turn up anything out of the ordinary on the property, and so the couple prepared for bed. Before Hugh Palliser could turn in, he heard the shed door open once again. Determined to catch what he now presumed was a prankster, Palliser stood quietly waiting for the door to open again. It did, but once again, the only thing to come into the room was a strong gust of cold air. He made a thorough search of the building and the surrounding land, but found no intruders, nor any other possible cause for the bizarre occurrence.

A short time previously, either during the construction of the new school (or possibly as a result of a bridge cave-in) a container of human remains had been found nearby. One of the Pallisers' children had an interest in anatomy and had consequently been given the bones to study. Hugh reasoned that it was the spirit of that person who was suddenly haunting the house. He lifted the lid on the box of bones and he could swear that the skull was grinning back at him. Quickly, he closed the lid and carried the box well out onto the property. He dug a grave and reinterred the bones. Immediately, evenings at the former Craigflower School building became considerably calmer.

Hugh Palliser went to his own grave without telling anyone exactly where he'd buried the restless soul. Although he must have done so with the best of intentions, his keeping of this secret has since caused some concern. Craigflower School is now a museum, preserved by the provincial government and recognized as the oldest surviving school building in western Canada.

Jerry Clark, the resident caretaker, was relaxing one evening—much as Palliser was doing those many years before when he heard the woodshed door—when his dog suddenly began to react to the sound of voices from an adjacent room. Clark searched the entire house and the surrounding land, but could find no reasonable explanation for what he and his dog had both heard.

On other occasions, loud noises have been heard coming from inside the school when it's unoccupied. The school bells will occasionally, and for no apparent reason, ring loudly enough to shake the entire building.

What a shame that no one living today knows where the skeletal remains of the unhappy soul are hidden—perhaps another move might calm the restless spirit.

A Glimpse of the Past

In the early 1900s, Rusty Campbell travelled around most of northern British Columbia. He was able to support himself by trapping and mining. Although it was for the most part a meagre existence, at least it was his choice. Rusty's reminiscences indicate that he deemed that the freedom to explore the ruggedly beautiful country of the North was worth sacrificing what comforts might come with a more secure life.

After a few years, however, he did find the loneliness difficult to bear, so he was delighted to meet up with a like-minded fellow named Jimmy. One fall day, sometime between 1909 and the outbreak of the First World War, the two men headed off to stake out some traplines.

The pair poled, paddled and portaged their canoe northward from Prince George. After successfully clearing the rapids at Giscome, they went further north and east on the McGregor River until they found the combination that they'd been looking for: isolation and an abundance of wildlife. By spring they would have enough pelts to make them both wealthy men.

Although their individual prosperity was extremely important to both Rusty and Jimmy, so was their friendship. For this reason, they divided the area to be trapped as fairly as possible. After all, they were intent on exploiting the area, not each other. Rusty's allotment "followed a creek down the slope to where it eventually entered the main river ... within a stone's throw of a small island on which stood the remains of 'Surprise City.'"

On a frozen winter's morn many years ago, Rusty Campbell was treated to a look back through the curtain of time.

As Rusty explained, "this is really no city nor the ruins of a city, but rather the tumbledown ruins of some winter quarters, which had been constructed of logs years ago."

Whether by deduction or from actual information garnered at area trading posts, Rusty concluded that the buildings had been constructed by a surveying party in the early days of the 1900s. He described coming across "old cabins now half hidden in a heavy growth of mountain alder and young spruce and balsam trees" and added, perhaps optimistically, "I think even today the crumbling walls and old fireplaces could easily be found, although now thoroughly in ruins."

Scuttlebutt among the trappers indicated that there was something decidedly unusual about this abandoned settlement. Rusty himself noted that he had heard "curious tales ... of canoe parties making a landing at the beach on [that island] at the dead of night, [and of people hearing] voices of men but when they hurried down to the landing to give a greeting there was only the gurgling river and murmuring dark spruce to return it." He also knew that the surveying party that had built the structures on the island "had packed up, glad to leave the lonely island."

One cold winter's day, Rusty was out checking his traps when he realized that it was getting dark and that he was too far from his base camp to make it back safely. He knew that he'd have to create a shelter in which to pass the night. Fortunately, it was not numbingly cold that evening and the river was not even completely frozen over. As an additional factor in Rusty's favour, he gratefully noted that there didn't seem to be a storm brewing. The most imposing force of nature that Rusty expected that he might have to contend with was the wind blowing the deep snow about. Feeling as contented as possible under the circumstances, he made himself something to eat, arranged his bedroll and soon fell asleep.

"I was awakened … a short time later … by the sound of voices … and the banging of canoe paddles against the side of a canoe frame. Thinking I was dreaming I threw back my sleeping robe and sat up. Little could be seen towards the river or island as a gusty snow curtain was driving down the valley. I clearly heard the sound of paddles and poles being thrown on the beach as if a landing was to be made. Suddenly the snow wrack [obscuring curtain] blew aside and I saw what looked like a party of canoe men disembarking on the beach. It was not till I had returned to the snugness of my sleeping robe that it dawned on me that a canoe could hardly come up a frozen river and that a stony beach four feet under packed snow could hardly be expected to give out the sound of wooden paddles being tossed on it."

Fascinated, Rusty Campbell continued to watch the drama that was apparently unfolding before his eyes.

"They seemed to be unloading camp gear and what looked like long musket-like firearms from their canoe. Two of them carrying what may have been an axe climbed the low bank and disappeared among the trees. A voice with a decided Scottish accent seemed to be calling instructions and was answered several times in soft French-Canadian patois but the distance and the wind prevented me from distinguishing any words."

Rusty Campbell continued to describe the strange sight. "One man in a dark fringed skin coat was handed a crutch as he painfully climbed out of the canoe and sat himself down … with every indication of extreme weariness or pain. I had just decided I should rouse myself and throw fresh wood on my … fire … as an indication of my presence when the whole scene became blotted out with a gust of heavy driving snow."

Rather than wait for the wind to die down so that he could go visit the newcomers, Campbell decided to go back to sleep and to greet the men in the morning. As he drifted back to sleep he "could hear the dull sound of chopping and the occasional murmur of voices through the storm. One man sang a snatch of what seemed like a French-Canadian shanty and then there was silence from the voyagers' camp."

He continued, "In the morning, after getting my fire going again, I noted about a half foot of new snow had fallen during the night. No sign of morning smoke was seen towards the strangers' camp but nevertheless I strapped on my snowshoes and went across the narrow strip of ice channel to investigate. There was no sign of a canoe, no half-filled tracks in the snow of any persons making a landing or climbing the bank and no sign of any person having made a camp on the island during the night. I turned to the stretch of open water below the island and snowshoed along its margin to where it dipped under the thick ice. It was scarce fifty paces long and the ice bridge at its close was at least eighteen inches thick. It had not formed during the night, that was certain. There was no open water as far as I could see above the island!"

Shaken by what he'd seen—or, more correctly, hadn't seen—Rusty Campbell made his way back to the area where he'd camped the previous night. He ends his report by suggesting that the reader might be at least as well equipped to come up with an explanation as was he, the witness to the strange event.

Although Rusty had no explanation for what had appeared before him that night about a century ago, it would be a safe bet to speculate that he had experienced retrocognition, that he had seen a ghostly replay of an event that had actually taken place some years previous.

Portrait Possessed

The following story comes from Chilliwack, which is near the eastern end of the Fraser Valley, a few hours' drive eastward from Vancouver. It is such a classic tale that it virtually supplies a dictionary definition of the phrase "haunted house." In addition, there is a chilling twist to this ghost story that is virtually guaranteed to raise a few extra goosebumps.

The year was 1965 and the Fredrickson family was delighted to be moving into a large old home, complete with a dramatic turret, on Williams Street. Hetty Fredrickson, a painter, looked forward to having room to pursue her craft while her husband, Douglas, was at work and their five children were at school. What Hetty ended up painting in the new house was very different, in all ways, from what she had intended.

The couple first noticed that not all was normal in the twelve-room house shortly after moving in. Furniture in an unused upstairs bedroom would not stay as they had left it. An oversized bed moved mysteriously about the room and the drawers in a bureau stored in that room would always be found open.

With so many people living in the house, such activity might have been ignored, with each family member thinking that another was responsible for the changes. The Fredricksons, however, weren't allowed such a luxury, because they could hear a ghost walking about in areas of the house that were supposedly unoccupied—by corporeal beings, that is. When the ghost came close to them, they could smell a distinctive fragrance and even hear the ghost's breathing.

Although understandably disturbed to realize that they'd purchased a haunted house, the couple made the decision to stay on. It was then that Hetty's recurring nightmares began. She dreamed of a woman lying on a floor. Hetty sensed that the scene had taken place in the family's home and yet, oddly, she didn't recognize the particular area where the woman lay. Almost in contradiction to that confusion was the clarity with which she could see the image in her dream. The entity itself was so clear in Hetty's dream that she began to paint the person that she had seen in her dream. Using her artistic talents, she tried to replicate the dream image: the mummified-looking body, the cheap, yellow-and-red cotton house dress and the look of terror on the face.

Little did Hetty suspect that this painting would only complicate the mystery further. Each day she would add to the woman's picture, but she soon discovered that the portrait had taken on a life of its own. It began changing overnight as the artist slept. Each morning she would find that the painting looked less and less like a woman and more and more like a man. One morning the image on the canvas had even "grown" a moustache!

Word of the strange goings-on in the Williams Street home began to spread, not only through the community, but throughout the Fraser Valley and beyond. People started to arrive at the door of the haunted house in droves. The Fredricksons did not appreciate all this attention suddenly being paid to them, but the ghost apparently did. It responded by gaining strength—sufficient strength to allow Hetty to see it not only in her nightmares, but also when she was awake. The sighting began as a glowing mist that then solidified into a discernible shape—the shape of a human body. Each time it appeared, the apparition soon faded, leaving behind a lingering scent of perfume.

Anxious to understand the problem that they were living with, the Fredricksons began to research the history of the house that they had just bought. Though they weren't able to come up with anything specific, they did discover that there were a lot of rumours in the community about that big old house on Williams Street. And none of those rumours were pleasant stories. Some said that a man had killed himself in the house; others had heard that a woman had been murdered there and that her killer had disposed of the remains by cementing them into the chimney.

At least now the Fredricksons felt that they had a clue as to why their house was haunted. They began to investigate room by room, looking for the concealed body. Their efforts were rewarded in that the couple found that the house was even bigger and more interesting than they'd originally thought. Tearing down a false wall revealed a boarded-up bedroom that they hadn't been aware of. Although neither of the Fredricksons had ever seen the area before, Hetty recognized it immediately—it was where the body in her dream lay.

During all of this investigation, Hetty continued to work on the portrait that she had started to paint. The moustache was slowly disappearing as mysteriously as it had appeared. Even so, the picture refused to look like a woman, for now it showed the outline of a beard.

Word of the strange goings on in Chilliwack had been picked up by the media and spread throughout the world. The Fredricksons allowed two journalists to spend the night in what had been the hidden bedroom. The ghost did not make itself visible to the reporters, but there were unexplainable noises throughout their stay and a piece of linoleum moved of its own accord.

After the two had filed their report, the haunted house became something of a provincial tourist attraction. Much to their chagrin, the Fredricksons now had to deal with curious tourists flocking to their door, in addition to the original inherent disadvantages of living in a haunted house. Finally everyone in the family had had enough. They packed up. They not only left the haunted house, they left the mainland entirely.

Once they were settled on Vancouver Island, the family tried to put the whole unpleasant experience out of their minds. Meanwhile, the Chilliwack house stood empty for months and became a target for vandals. To prevent further disintegration, the Fredricksons invited a group of musicians to move in and live there as long as they liked. The group did not even have to pay any rent as long as they cared for the house. The musicians were more than happy to comply with that simple request and carefully maintained the property. All of them were well aware that they were living in a place reputed to be haunted, and yet not one of them ever had an unusual experience in the house.

Eventually the Fredricksons sold the place, the musicians moved out, and a new family moved in. The strange occurrences began all over again. Doors and drawers would bang closed. The thermostat would be set ten degrees higher than anyone in the earthly family was comfortable with. They felt decidedly uncomfortable in the basement of the house and their pet dog occasionally shook and cowered as though frightened by something that no human could see. When the children in this household began to experience night terrors, the parents decided to cut their losses and moved out.

After they moved, the old place on Williams Street was vacant more often than occupied, but even the lack of inhabitants did not stop new ghost stories from surfacing. People spoke of an unexplained shadow moving about the house. A courier approaching the house to deliver a parcel was startled to see a woman holding a baby suddenly appear on the front porch and then just as suddenly disappear.

There seemed to be no solution to this ongoing haunting. The house was either up for sale or unoccupied for many of the following years. No one, it seemed, could stand living there for very long. Then, in the mid-1970s, a fire of unknown origin started in the cellar of the haunted house. Soon flames engulfed the entire structure and the place burned to the ground—taking its supernatural secrets with it.

The Phantom Carriage

Kelowna's Guisachan Ranch has a long and romantic past. The house was built in the 1890s for Governor General Lord Aberdeen. The property was named after Lady Aberdeen's childhood home in Scotland. Reports indicate that, until just a few years ago, it was the site of an unusual haunting.

Every so often, the wheels of a phantom carriage rolling along the gravel driveway and the *clip-clop* of phantom horses' hooves could be heard approaching the house. Then the sounds would cease for a few moments, as though the buggy had stopped for the passengers to get out. Moments later, the sounds would start up again, this time retreating, and yet no one saw a carriage and no guests arrived at the house.

No one knows when the phantom carriage began arriving, but local legend has it that the original carriage was carrying guests to a party that Lord and Lady Aberdeen were hosting. Perhaps tragedy struck the little group on the way and their souls were doomed to repeat that final journey for decades and decades to come.

Many people have witnessed the phenomenon and nearly as many have investigated it, hoping to find an explanation for the mysterious sounds or, at the very least, to see something. There have been no reports ever of an apparition being seen, but the auditory manifestation was heard over and over again through the years.

Elaine Cameron, who enjoyed a lengthy residency on the property, suggested that the flat land surrounding the ranch would allow sound from a carriage on the nearby road to travel unobstructed toward the house until the vehicle was in such a position that the sound waves were blocked by the rows of trees along the driveway. "Just long enough to give the impression of a rig having stopped," she explained. The sounds would then pick up again once the carriage had moved far enough so that the trees no longer blocked them.

That explanation is certainly an interesting one and, in the days of travel by horse and carriage, it might even have made sense. When the sounds of the phantom horse-drawn buggy were still being

A phantom carriage was for many years heard approaching Guisachan House.

heard for years after the advent of the automobile, that explanation became as puzzling as the sounds themselves.

These phantom presences were very much a part of the site for many years. However, according to George Rieder, who currently owns and operates the restaurant at Guisachan House, the ghosts that haunted the place for so long may at last have gone on to their final reward.

Haunted Hat Creek Ranch

Hat Creek Ranch, located on the Cariboo Wagon Road, built between New Westminster and Barkerville (see Chapter 2), had already had a long and colourful history even before it became a stopping place for miners on their way to strike it rich. The land where the ranch is now, and its surroundings, had previously been used as Hudson's Bay Company pastureland. By the late 1860s, it had been settled by those with an eye to exploiting the thousands of fortune-seekers who'd be passing through.

Business boomed and by 1872 an entrepreneur had constructed a road-house to provide travellers with food and overnight accommodation. However, the venture was perhaps not as safe an endeavour as the owner might have hoped it would be. By the time that the fortune-seekers reached the Hat Creek area, any who were

Hat Creek Ranch, near Cache Creek, is one of British Columbia's most haunted spots.

not a tough sort to begin with had certainly become that way. Fights and brawls were everyday occurrences and it's unlikely that much attention was paid to a formal justice system when settling disagreements. This was, after all, the Wild West.

Such a traumatic past has left psychic scars on the buildings at Hat Creek Ranch, scars that can still be seen, heard and felt today—in the form of ghosts. The very haunted ranch is a provincial historic site and, as such, receives visitors from all over the world every year. Many of those tourists report that their visit was especially memorable because they encountered at least one paranormal presence.

Not all of these paranormal encounters left those who'd experienced them feeling warm and comforted, however. The footsteps that are heard on the second floor of the former roadhouse are usually followed by the sounds of doors slamming. Moments later, a female voice has been heard crying out for help. The voice may have been a ghostly reverberation belonging to a manifestation that has been seen on more than one occasion in a particular upstairs room. The apparition, an elderly woman with her hair tied up in a neat bun, apparently sits knitting in a rocking chair. This ghost may be the same one that was seen by a worker after hearing footsteps travelling along a hallway. When he looked out of his office to see who was there, he was only able to catch a glimpse of black-and-white apparel before the image, and the sounds, vanished.

Much scarier, the presence on the back stairs has been neither seen nor heard, but it is one of the most dreaded spirits at Hat Creek Ranch. It causes people to feel that their safety is in jeopardy, as it creates the sense that they are about to be pushed down the stairs.

On the lower level of the building, glasses in the bar area move about mysteriously, as do solid blocks of wood that have been carefully placed to serve as doorstops. Many folks have reported something tugging at their clothing at the same time as a chilly and unexplainable draft wafts past them.

People have also had experiences on the property surrounding the ranch buildings. In the barn, horses have been observed becoming distressed at the sound of coughing—but the animals' reaction is most understandable, given that no such distinctive sound had come from any live person present.

Outside, the phantom hoofbeats of long-dead horses are routinely heard trotting along the road before turning and making their way into the barn. Perhaps there the ghost-horses will be re-shod by the ghost of the blacksmith. His hammer is often heard clanking on metal, accompanied by the hissing of air escaping from the bellows used to fan the flames of the forge.

A worker who was living with his family at the ranch was not the least bit concerned when his preschool-age daughter acquired what he took to be an imaginary playmate. One day when the family was outside, however, the man's composure was shaken. There, in front of one of the buildings, just for an instant, appeared the image of a little girl. As his eyes struggled to make sense of the sight, his ears were attending to his little daughter's excited voice—advising her parents, "There's my friend!" while pointing at the tiny entity.

The most gruesome ghost at Hat Creek is in the granary. History records that a man hanged himself there many years ago. Today, the vision of the lifeless body can still be seen dangling from the rafters at the end of his home-made executioner's noose.

It would seem that perhaps the entire ranch property continues to feel the effects of its tragic past.

Three Old Ghost Stories

When he died in 1954 at the age of ninety-two, retired railroad employee Matthew Fulton Crawford took a piece of history with him. He was the last remaining survivor of those who had attended the ceremonial driving of the Canadian Pacific Railway's Last Spike in 1885. Fortunately for ghost story lovers everywhere, he left behind accounts of a few of his stranger experiences while working along that first ribbon of steel that connected our country from sea to sea.

These stories have become legendary among railway crews as proof that the bond among them extends beyond the world that the rest of us know.

In the spring of 1895, Crawford was piloting his steam train from Kamloops southward to North Bend, which is about midway between Lytton and Yale. Much to the entire crew's relief, the trip had been uneventful so far. The section of track that they were just about to leave led through some dangerous curves with steep drop-offs. In addition, it was common for patches of that section to be blocked by avalanches, mudslides or fallen boulders.

On this particular day, just as the sun set to the west, a heavy rain began to fall. In unspoken agreement, the crew's level of vigilance picked up as the skies darkened above them. Crawford and his fireman exchanged simple, nearly meaningless, acknowledgements about the weather as they continued about their duties. They'd all been through far worse weather but, despite the apparent ordinariness of the situation, Crawford found himself becoming inexplicably apprehensive. His nerves were too taut to continue anything even resembling banter with his trusted and long-standing partner, the fireman. They worked on in silence until a voice screamed, "Stop! Don't go any further!"

Whirling around in his chair, engineer Crawford screamed back, "Why? What do you see?"

"Nothing," came the surprised-looking fireman's reply, for the warning had not been his and he hadn't heard it.

"Why did you order me to stop, then?" Crawford demanded in a high-pitched, stressed-sounding voice.

"I didn't say anything, Matt. Relax. You're letting your nerves get the best of you. Everything's all right," the fireman advised.

Not content this time to take his partner's word for it, Matthew Crawford thrust his head out the cab window. Although he could see nothing in the inky blackness, he certainly heard something. It was that voice again. This time, it was shouting even louder—only one word, over and over again, "Stop! Stop! Stop!"

Unable to disregard these clear instructions, Matthew Crawford applied the brakes as abruptly as he felt was safe.

"What are you doing, Matt? We're making good time. Don't throw us off schedule," the fireman tried to reason with the nearly panicked engineer.

As the train ground to a complete halt, Crawford grabbed a lantern and jumped down from his cab. By this time, the crew from the cars further back in the train had made their way forward to ask what was going on.

"He's hearing voices," the fireman said, with a disparaging gesture toward the engineer out on the tracks. As their curiosity had been aroused and, since there was nothing to be gained by staying in the train, two of the crew joined Matt Crawford out on the tracks. Moments later the trio stood stock-still and stared in disbelief. There, just ahead, a rockslide had ripped the track to shreds. Below roared the mighty Fraser River. It would have been certain death to all on board had Matthew Crawford not obeyed the phantom voice's instructions.

The supernatural presence that warned the engineer of the danger ahead didn't make itself visible that night, but it didn't have to, for it had made itself heard. More importantly, its advice had been heeded, but just in time.

The next year, Matthew Crawford had another psychic experience in almost exactly the same spot, but this time while he was heading his train eastward toward Kamloops.

By coincidence, on this night Crawford's brother-in-law, a young man named John Ladner, was his fireman. In this instance, it was not Crawford, but the fireman, who was suffering the sense of impending doom, in grave contradiction to the man's usually upbeat mood.

The trip was progressing uneventfully until, without warning, the emergency signal sounded loudly throughout the line of cars from caboose to engine. It could mean only one thing—somehow a break had occurred somewhere in the train. It seemed a strange point in the route for such a thing to occur, but all the experienced hands on board were grateful that, if it had to happen, at least it had happened at this point in the trip. Just ahead was a particularly dangerous stretch.

The engineer began to slow the train in preparation for fixing the problem. However, when the crew members tried to sort out among themselves just who it was that had pulled the cord to sound the alarm—or discover where the supposed break was—no one knew anything about it. After checking all the freight cars for any possible stowaways, the group came to the conclusion that they'd suffered some sort of a mass auditory hallucination and had just *thought* that they'd heard the alarm. All of the crew members resumed their positions in the train but, just as Matthew Crawford reached for the throttle to bring the train back up to speed, the alarm sounded a second time.

"Stop, Matt," his brother-in-law screamed, before crying, "Jump—we're going to hit!"

Knowing better than to question what was happening, Matthew Crawford followed directly on Jack Ladner's heels. Seconds later, the cab crashed into a pile of rocks that blocked the tunnel entrance just ahead. Both Crawford and Ladner were injured and the rest of the crew were shaken up but, thanks to an unseen entity that had twice sounded the alarm gong, at least no one had been killed.

It was some time before Jack Ladner was well enough to return to work but, once he did return, he was happiest when he was back in partnership with his brother-in-law, Matthew Crawford. On the evening of Thursday, January 21, 1904, although they were not working together, they anticipated seeing one another. Crawford would be in his passenger train and Ladner was assigned to an auxiliary engine responsible for providing additional power to any train that needed help reaching the Rogers Pass summit in the Rockies. Their schedules indicated that they'd be in the station at Field at the same time.

The two men greeted each other warmly. Crawford proudly showed Jack a watch that he'd just purchased and explained that its accuracy was guaranteed for life. Because Matthew Crawford intended to use the watch for work, he had chosen one that used the twenty-four-hour clock, to correspond to railroad schedules. After the timepiece had been duly admired and discussed, the two exchanged information about the terrible winter storm that seemed to be brewing all about the area. As the older of the pair, Matt Crawford took it upon himself to advise Jack of the possible safety measures that the younger man might want to avail himself of as he traversed steep inclines in a raging blizzard.

Jack acknowledged his friend's well-meant words and assured him there was no need to worry. Not only was Jack confident about his own abilities, he was confident about the equipment that he was charged with operating. As they bid each other a good night, Jack called out "If I don't get there safely, I'll find a way to let you know."

"Forget that! Just be careful," Crawford admonished before climbing into his cab seat and heading out on the next leg of his run.

Once the trip was under way, Crawford and his crew ate a hearty meal. The engineer took out his new watch to show it around for all to admire. After bragging about its reputedly accurate timekeeping qualities, he was shocked to notice that it wasn't reading the correct time at all. The watch was stopped at 19:56—four minutes before eight o'clock in the evening.

While the sounds of his crew's teasing faded into the background Matt Crawford carefully inspected his newly purchased timepiece. He tried to wind it, he tried to adjust it, but nothing did any good.

The watch continued to read 19:56. Concerned now that the implications of the stopped watch were more ominous than anything to do with its quality, Crawford stared straight ahead and said nothing until they reached the next station on the line.

There, a terrible message awaited him. Jack's engine had met with a dreadful accident. Despite the younger man's experience and care, as well as the safety features incorporated into both the track and the engine, the engine had plummeted out of control off the tracks and into a boulder. There was no sign of either Jack or the fireman.

It took an experienced rescue party three days before they found the bodies in the mangled remains. The searchers discovered that the glass covers on Jack's watch and the clock in the engine had both shattered with the impact and that both devices had stopped at exactly four minutes before eight o'clock in the evening—precisely the same time that Matthew's new watch had frozen.

Crawford slowly realized exactly what had happened: Just as he had promised, Jack Ladner had sent his beloved brother-in-law a final message by stopping that new watch at the precise moment of his own death. For those three days while Jack's body was missing, all three timepieces—Jack's watch, the clock in the cab of the wrecked engine and Matthew Crawford's new watch—had read exactly the same time.

As salvage crews disassembled the twisted remains of the wreck, the hands of the clock inside began to move. Matthew Crawford removed Jack Ladner's watch from his body, set the time correctly and wound it. To Crawford's utter amazement, the mechanism functioned as though nothing had happened. Crawford's own watch, however, the one that he'd just recently purchased and that had been so highly recommended by the jeweller, never worked again. The hands remained frozen at 19:56.

From that day onward, Matthew Crawford wore Jack Ladner's watch, but he also kept his own broken one for the rest of his life. He never wavered from his conviction that, as his brother-in-law's spirit was leaving its earthly body, it had stopped his new watch as a sign.

A Bizarre Old Story

One of the oldest ghost stories in Canada took place on the old Cariboo Trail, or Cariboo Wagon Road, between Yale and Lillooet. The road was completed in 1864, but the route saw little traffic for the first few years. Many of those who did travel that way were never heard from again. It seems that the route was haunted by a vengeful phantom. Little is left in the way of documentation for this old and bizarre ghost story, but what information has been passed down is enough to let anyone know that supernatural forces were at work.

The story begins with a man named John Fillmore, who was leading a team of men and mules along the trail. They were taking supplies to miners and had made their way as far as Spences Bridge by the time night fell on August 5, 1863. The group, consisting of a dozen men and fifty pack animals, made camp for the night. They ate a hearty dinner, appointed guards to stand watch, and then turned in for the night.

The next morning, Fillmore asked the guards if anything untoward had happened through the night. He was told that, shortly after the men and mules fell asleep, a strange white light had appeared in the sky but, other than that, there had been no unusual events. Fillmore barely had time to contemplate what the light that the man had seen could possibly have been before another of his party approached him in obvious distress. It seemed that some of the mules were missing.

In a separate incident three nights later and closer to Yale, George Lateau and his party were making their way with a group of pack-mules. The beasts were loaded down with nuggets of gold that Lateau and the others had just mined. That night, the newly wealthy men noted strange white lights in the sky moving in a semicircle. By the next morning, some of their mules had vanished.

Not connecting these ghost lights with the animals' disappearance, the men began to question one another before heading out to try to find the missing mules. The beasts had to be somewhere, they reasoned. They could not simply have vanished. Lateau's men searched the area carefully. They could not find the mules, nor any trace that anyone had sneaked into their camp to steal the animals and their loads.

This bizarre scenario of strange lights in the sky followed by missing mules was repeated over and over again throughout 1863 until, by the fall of that year, the route was rarely used. As the British Columbia government of the day had gone to a great deal of expense in order to build the trail, the authorities were most interested in making sure that it was being used.

The fledgling Pinkerton Detective Agency was called in to help solve the mystery. They leaked word to the press that a mule train carrying $50,000 in gold would soon be making its way up the trail. It was a ruse. All the "miners" on this trek were actually Pinkerton detectives and they had no gold in their packs. The trip was merely a ploy to draw out the supposed "phantom" of the Cariboo Trail and to make the route seem more appealing to other travellers.

The impostors slept even less than they'd planned to. Although they'd plotted out guarding schedules so that several men would be awake at all times, the investigators whose turn it was to sleep found that they weren't able to. Spectral lights kept everyone awake almost all of the time. Despite all the precautions, three mules somehow disappeared.

The mystery continued for all of 1863 and into 1864. By 1865, however, the ghost lights in the night skies and the thefts of mules simply stopped as quickly as they had begun. Usage of the trail increased and it began to serve as many people as the government had hoped it would.

To this day, no one has any idea of what invisible presence haunted the Cariboo Trail for those few months, nor was any trace of the dozens of missing pack animals ever found. The mule-stealing spirit from the early days of European settlement in this province was apparently working according to its own agenda and timetable.

Chapter 8

GHOSTS IN PUBLIC

The following stories provide, in my opinion, some of the most convincing evidence that ghosts do exist. It seems to me that when hundreds of people, over several decades, witness an apparition or other sign of a ghostly presence in a certain place, those encounters are difficult to dismiss.

The Siwash Sightings

The "dark and stormy night" has a long, and well-deserved, reputation as a traditional setting for a scary story. Although nocturnal turbulence is undeniably a provocative context, surely the inherent eeriness of predawn stillness is equally suggestive for a ghostly sighting. Indeed, it was that latter situation that provided the setting for a series of frightening sightings in the Siwash Cemetery near the city of Courtenay on the east side of Vancouver Island.

Three sailors who saw the cemetery apparition while on shore leave were petrified—frozen on the spot in fear. They huddled together at the side of the road in terror until sun-up and then steadfastly refused to discuss even among themselves the vision that they'd been witness to, until much later.

A number of community members who also saw the manifestation were likewise initially unwilling to share information about their experience with anyone but their closest confidants. Once people began to talk about what they had seen, word spread quickly. During the Christmas season of 1940 and continuing until just after New Year's Day, 1941, the story of this Island ghost made headlines all over Canada.

The first person amenable to being identified in connection with this ghost story was a sceptic named Bill Spurrill. He at least acknowledged that he had indeed seen something most extraordinary.

Spurrill had been thoroughly intrigued by the floating image that he had seen in the cemetery and had stopped to watch it for some time. He readily admitted that the manifestation resembled a human being, but he added that the way the mysterious shape moved and undulated indicated that it could not possibly have been a person.

Later in the day, Spurrill confirmed for excited journalists that he'd watched the strange form "straddling the road ahead of him." As he stared, the "white swaying shape ... took on a green glow ... and then dissolved."

The other witness willing to be interviewed after sighting the phantom was a Comox resident named William Day. Like Spurrill, Day was a sceptic. He was quoted as saying, "I have always laughed at ghosts and things of that kind." Despite this bias, Day described the apparition in detail, noting that he had the advantage of carrying a lamp at the time that the image appeared.

Initially, the spectre appeared as a white form about 7 metres (20 feet) ahead of Day. The vision moved toward him in "a sort of a dance step" before disappearing, literally in the blink of an eye. The startled man stood still for a moment, trying to make some sense out of what he'd just seen, before continuing on his way. As he stared, an image "of a woman came out of nowhere," he told a journalist. Thinking that someone was making sport of him, William Day approached the manifestation, which vanished as he stared at it.

Perhaps because they were both sceptics, neither of these two men were terrified by their experiences the way the sailors were. Day did not offer an explanation for the strange vision that he'd observed. Spurrill decided that since the sightings were occurring just before dawn, what had really been seen was simply a mist, with colour changes caused by phosphorescence picked up from the nearby sea spray.

No doubt such vapours have, on occasion, been misinterpreted as paranormal phenomena. In this case, however, Bill's "rational" explanation seems to strain credibility farther than merely accepting the existence of ghosts. Surely, if the sightings had been misidentified sea mists, they would have continued on, even until today, but the spectre vanished for the last time after the first week in 1941, and it has never been seen again.

Phantoms in Field

In Yoho National Park, about a half-hour's drive west of the famous Rocky Mountain attraction of Lake Louise, is the town of Field, British Columbia. Field is no ghost town. Far from it. Field is a bustling community full of vibrant, active individuals. But it is also full of ghosts.

Cemeteries are not as often haunted as people think that they might be, but the graveyard in Field is "alive" with ghosts. Most visitors to the enclosure can feel the spirits' presence. On one occasion, a young First Nations man was physically unable to enter the area. He reported feeling a wall of energy holding him back.

In another incident, an employee with Parks Canada reported that the first time he had to go into the cemetery to obtain water samples he felt extremely uncomfortable, as though he was being closely watched, almost scrutinized. Nevertheless, he attended to the matter that he had to and then left as quickly as possible. It wasn't until he was a good distance away from the graves that the hairs on the back of his neck finally lay back down.

Although he didn't see anything in the way of either an apparition or ghost lights, he's since decided that whatever spirits were residing in the place were somehow testing him. As the man has never felt the same foreboding in the place since that incident, he presumes that the entities found him acceptable.

And then there's the ghost of the cowboy that is frequently seen in various places in Field. Sometimes the manifestation is alone and at other times it is with two other ghosts.

A Reiki master, who is sensitive to these sorts of things, indicates that it is Field's location on "some sort of an energy vortex" that has given rise to all the supernatural activity in the town. At a possibly much more mundane level, Field is nestled in a valley and surrounded closely by high mountains, which results in the town experiencing some of the most severe weather conditions in Canada. And perhaps these weather conditions build such a strong desire to survive that the spirits of the deceased don't want to give up and move on, even long after their bodies have died.

Mournful Sounds Still Heard

Kevin McDermid arrived in British Columbia in the late 1860s, temporarily leaving his wife at home in Scotland. He worked in the mines between Hope and Princeton, desperately trying to amass sufficient funds to get settled and send for his beloved.

In 1869, with McDermid still well short of his financial goal, there was a terrible explosion at the mine where he worked. Although he survived the blast, one of his legs was blown off. He would never work as a miner again. Not knowing what else to do, he wrote to his wife. Not only did he need her to nurse him back to health, but also to help him cope.

Mrs. McDermid arrived in the extraordinarily beautiful southwestern British Columbian countryside and, as best they were able, the couple made a home for themselves. The spot that they chose was very isolated. They lived there for many years. One of Kevin McDermid's greatest pleasures was to make his way up into the hills carrying his bagpipes. There he would play mournful melodies to the wide open spaces, rugged peaks and deep valleys.

When Mrs. McDermid took ill one year, Kevin tried frantically to save her. Despite his determined efforts, the woman died. Kevin grieved terribly and became quite reclusive. The years passed by. When nearby townsfolk, who were used to seeing the eccentric Scotsman at least a few times a year, noticed that he hadn't made his usual trek into town for supplies, they became concerned and organized a party to check on Kevin, who was by this time an old man.

As the group approached the small, ramshackle abode, they knew that all was not well, for the lifeless body of the man's horse lay on the ground, still tethered to a tree near the house. Further into the woods, they found the remains of McDermid's bagpipes. They

These hills are still occasionally alive with the sounds of phantom bagpipe music.

searched throughout the area, but never found the man, his corpse or any clue as to what might have happened.

Locals say that, on a clear night, you can still hear the melancholy strains of a lover's lament played on the bagpipes. Some people even claim that they've seen the phantom lone piper as he chanted an ode to his long-deceased beloved.

The Wraith of the Kandahar

Despite numerous attempts to do so, I've been unable to validate the authenticity of this ghost story. Even though the tale *may* be a work of fiction, I have decided to include it in this collection. At the very least it is an enchanting legend and, in light of similar stories that I've been told, it is more than possible that the following events did happen just exactly as the journalist who wrote the story for the *Vancouver Sun Magazine* in January 1949 said that they did.

On a chilly Friday evening during January 1938, a group of skiers gathered to socialize in the Chalet high atop Grouse Mountain, just to the north across Burrard Inlet from downtown Vancouver. It was a beautiful clear night. Moonlight reflected against the deep blanket of fresh snow, making the areas that were bare of trees nearly as bright as day. The most challenging ski runs are those that work their way through stands of trees so dense that direct sunlight cannot penetrate to the trails. The Kandahar was no exception.

Everyone who had gathered around the roaring fire in the Chalet's fireplace was looking forward to a full weekend of skiing. Friendly wagers were exchanged as to who would be the first one down the Kandahar run in the morning. It was considered an honour to be the one to blaze the twisting, turning trail of pristine white powder. The importance of this friendly rivalry meant that all but the diehard partiers retreated to their beds early that night. Everyone wanted to be refreshed for a full Saturday of skiing, and possibly even awake early enough to claim the first swoosh down the mountain.

By midnight, only a handful of partiers were left in the central cabin. Those few who remained on that magical night were rewarded with a sight that they'll never forget. First one person and then another caught a glimpse of a darkened silhouette as it skied past the Chalet window. Amazed at what they thought they'd seen, the members of the little group ran to the door and out onto the deck. They stared in wonderment and disbelief as they watched the figure of a skier swoosh down the mountainside at breakneck speed toward the trail through the forest.

"Impossible!" was the first word spoken by the witnesses. "Fifty miles an hour [80 kilometres per hour] into blind blackness?" uttered an astonished spectator. Surely no one would be foolhardy enough to try the Kandahar run at night, they thought. Why, the entire length of the trail was dotted with trees marked by "X"s—a skiers' sign that someone had not safely navigated around that natural obstacle. Logic dictated that no one would attempt to ski that slope at night, but what the group had seen contradicted that reasoning: not only had they seen the skier for themselves just minutes ago, but the ski tracks remained behind, cut clearly into the powder.

By the next morning, word of the incredible sighting had spread among the rest of the skiers on the mountain. Several people who had been out walking at the edge of the 1.6-kilometre (1-mile) long run late that night also reported having seen the phantom skier. They all confirmed that he was not carrying a lantern and yet his tracks, readily visible in Saturday morning's daylight, indicated that the entity had successfully made his way to the ski village at the bottom of the mountain—an accomplishment that no human being could ever hope to make. What so many credible witnesses had seen simply could not have happened—unless, like so many other ski hills, Grouse Mountain was haunted.

The Ghost Riders

It was an August day in 1984 and Harold McDougall and his son, Gary, a photographer from Penticton, were enjoyably exploring the remote terrain around Elinor Lake near Naramata in the province's Okanagan Valley just south of Kelowna. While stopped for a trailside lunch, the pair felt totally isolated from the world as they savoured their food and appreciated the peaceful quiet of their surroundings.

To their great surprise, the two men heard the distinctive sounds of horses' hooves approaching along the trail. Moments later, a group of five riders appeared in a nearby clearing. The two oldest, the McDougalls surmised, might have been the parents of the three younger ones.

All the riders were dressed in clothing that was far too heavy for a warm summer's day. The men wore cloth hats, suspenders to hold up their heavyweight trousers, and high riding boots. Their horses' saddles were simple, adorned only by the heavy canvas bags strapped to them. The vision that the McDougalls cast their eyes upon that day was undeniably a strange one. The approaching family's odd appearance was certainly no reason for rudeness, so Harold called out a greeting.

This simple gesture appeared to startle the travellers. When the man that the two hikers presumed to be the father of the younger three riders regained his composure, he touched his hat briefly in acknowledgement before quickly leading his little group away from the two men.

As the group of riders slowly came past the father and son who'd been enjoying their trailside lunch, the pair noted something most unusual: silence. The family riding past at a trot seemed enveloped in a casing of total silence, a silence so complete that it absorbed the surrounding sounds of leaves rustling and birds chirping, and even the gurgling of a nearby brook.

More than a little intrigued, Harold and Gary waited just a moment before attempting to follow the family, if only to get a second look that might somehow confirm what they'd just seen. They hurried to the trail, which was as straight as an arrow at that point. Although they could see clearly for a considerable distance in either direction, they could spot no trace of either the five people or their horses.

Stranger still, as the McDougalls walked along the dirt trail, they noted that their own steps left footprints on the ground, but there was no sign of any prints from horses' hooves. They then realized what, other than being excessive for the weather, was odd about the family's clothing: it was of a style from a much earlier era. For just a moment, apparently, Gary and Harold McDougall were privy to a peek backward, through the curtain of time.

On a farm not far from Elinor Lake, but many years before the incident described above, two brothers left their house on a snowy winter evening to attend to their chores. When Sam and Edward Richards were finished tending to the horses in the barn, they came outside and noticed a man walking toward them. The lads saw the image clearly and later described it as having been dressed all in white.

Their farmstead home was in the rolling foothills and extremely isolated, so this sight struck both boys as being very odd. Thinking that the man had lost his way, they called out to him, but they got no response. The image merely continued along the path up to the Richardses' house. The boys followed it—or tried to, for seconds later the man that they'd both distinctly seen vanished.

Sam and Edward rushed in to tell their parents of the strange trespasser. Upon hearing their sons' news, Mr. and Mrs. Richards were just as concerned as the youngsters had been. They immediately bundled up and followed the boys out to the yard. There was no one there, nor were there any footprints in the snow.

At their parents' urging, the Richards boys described the white coat that the image had been wearing. It was finally clear then what had happened. Like the McDougalls in the previous story, the boys had had a firsthand look at the past. They had experienced retrocognition.

Psychic Tells All

Few venues are as public as a radio station phone-in show. In the late 1970s, when Vancouver on-air personality Terry Moore invited the very psychic Freda Fell to be a guest on his program, Lower Mainland listeners were treated to some fascinating other-worldly interviews.

Fell had apparently been clairvoyant as long as she could remember. She recalled that as a child living in England she thought that everyone could detect what other people were thinking and that everyone received communications from the dead. She frequently held what she thought were normal conversations with dead relatives. Over time she realized that her abilities were very special gifts and she began to train herself to act as a communications conduit both from the living to the dead and from the dead to the living. Her abilities were so strong and she honed them so carefully that by the time that she emigrated from England to British Columbia she was able to give amazingly accurate psychic readings—even over the telephone.

The first caller to Terry Moore's show was a woman. She had uttered only three words, "Good afternoon, Freda," when the medium began to intuit information about the caller. Fell "saw" with her mind's eye that the woman was wearing a blue ring. A voice in Fell's "inner ear," as she described it, told her that the caller was close to an elderly woman who was beginning to suffer from memory lapses. The information was amazingly accurate, as absolutely confirmed by the caller but, disappointingly for me, did not involve any contact with the souls of the dead. Neither did any of the other on-air conversations that day.

During an in-person session, however, Freda was able to help a young woman come to terms with her deceased grandmother, a person whom she'd held great resentment against.

No sooner had the meeting between "Gayle" (a pseudonym) and Freda begun, than Freda announced to Gayle that her paternal grandmother was present and very anxious to communicate with the younger woman. Gayle had come to Freda for information on other matters and her reaction to Freda's announcement was swift and most assuredly not positive.

Grandmother, it seemed, had made not only Gayle's existence miserable, but also that of her mother. The death of her father's mother had actually meant a relief from suffering for the other two women. Because of her resentment at the treatment that she had received at the hand of her grandmother, Gayle had no desire at all to interact with the deceased woman's spirit and initially would not even entertain hearing from her grandmother.

Finally the psychic insisted, "If you don't want your grandmother to speak to you, there is no use going any further. I have no control over the spirit friends or loved ones who want to come through me and I won't close the door to any of them. They each have the right to have their say. So, if you are opposed to your grandmother for some family reason, we might as well terminate this session right now."

Having heard the gifted woman's ultimatum, Gayle changed her mind and agreed to listen to the message from the spirit of her once-feared grandmother. Her agreement was a turning point in resolving issues that everyone in the family had thought insoluble. It seems that Gayle's grandmother had, after her death, realized how cruel she'd been to both her daughter-in-law and her granddaughter. She came through to Gayle via Freda to express her remorse and regret. As a result, hurts carried by both the living and the dead were at last cleared up.

An Enigmatic Escort

In the late 1920s, Frederick William Lindsay was a young man. Something of a dandy, Fred had been living the high life. He was drifting around British Columbia, thoroughly enjoying the cockiness of his youth, when the Great Depression came crashing down on him—and on most of the rest of the world.

The young man's life changed for the worse virtually overnight. Even so, he was considerably better off than many—at least he wasn't begging or riding the rails. A make-work project, jointly sponsored by both the provincial and federal governments, was created to construct the High Arrow Dam at Arrow Lake to increase its size. Fred, and dozens of other men, sought refuge from the Depression there. Although they were paid only seven dollars per month to work more hours per week than would probably be legal today, anyone who could get on at a work camp was considered fortunate, for they were neither starving nor homeless, as were many people in British Columbia through the Dirty Thirties.

Fred's easy spending ways didn't leave him as quickly as his money did. So, on a certain evening in November 1932, he found himself alone in the camp bunk-house, too broke to attend the local dance with his mates. Boredom soon set in. His mind wandered back over some of the more exciting evenings that he'd enjoyed in his life, in more prosperous times.

"Goodness knows what made me think of the glass of water and the crystal ball," Fred commented some thirty years after the fact. "But think of it I did."

Apparently, somewhere in his travels, someone had told Fred Lindsay that a simple glass of water could be used in place of a crystal ball. Given that such an experiment was one of the few diversions available to him at that moment, he decided to give it a try. He filled an ordinary kitchen tumbler full of water and set it on the table in front of him.

The coal-oil lamp gave off something of an eerie glow as Fred gazed into the glass of water. Mere seconds later, he began to feel foolish. What if any of his bunk-mates were to come home early and find him doing anything so silly? He'd never live it down. Their teasing would make his life miserable for months, Fred knew.

But then, just as he was about to abandon his trial, he noticed that the water in the glass was becoming cloudy. As he stared in disbelief, the plain tap water took on a milky quality. Fascinated by the bizarre changes that he was witnessing, Fred stared intently. At the centre of the cloudy liquid he thought that he saw a small dark area. Slowly, that nondescript dark patch resolved itself into the form of a tiny likeness of a person, a man. It was a man whom Fred Lindsay recognized. There before him was the image of his recently deceased friend, Jack McFarlane.

Fred peered more closely at the amazing sight. As the miniature figure in the cloud continued to become clearer and clearer, Fred became even more concerned. "Black Jack," as Fred had always called his friend, was dressed in a hooded robe. He was gesturing angrily toward Fred. The manifestation was furiously mouthing words.

"He shook his fists at me while apparently giving me a terrible calling down. But I could not hear him; I could only see him," Fred recalled.

Slowly, just as they had appeared, first the image and then the cloudiness of the liquid disappeared from the glass. The glass of water was once again just a plain glass of water but Fred was, understandably, a shaken man. Not knowing what he had done or what he should do about it, the man climbed into his bed and fell into a fitful sleep, not even awakening when his friends noisily made their way back from the dance. The next morning he did his best to put the entire experience out of his mind.

As New Year's Eve 1932 led to New Year's Day 1933, there wasn't much for Fred or anyone else to celebrate in the Arrow Lake work camp. Life continued on, with one boring day very much resembling the boring day that had gone before it. The last week of January, however, brought at least a bit of excitement to the restless young men. A trapper who was passing through stayed in the bunk-house for a few nights and entertained the isolated workers with tales of his trials and travels. He recounted many adventures, including one involving a miner whom he'd met on the north side of the Monashee Mountains and who'd been looking for a partner.

Fred Lindsay was just bored enough with the stultifying security of his situation to latch onto such a fragment of information. He immediately began making plans to leave the work camp and find that miner. The friends he'd made at the dam-building project tried their best to dissuade him.

"It's second-hand information, Fred. Don't risk what you have here for that," said one.

"It's winter. You'll never make it out of the valley alive," said another.

Their words were not news to Fred. He'd said them all to himself, with no effect. Scrounging what little food and supplies he could, on February 2, 1933, the restless young man set out to begin his foolhardy mission. His route was deeply covered in snow. He'd managed to salvage a pair of snowshoes but, as they were in poor repair and he had no experience walking with them, these supposed aids were initially a serious disadvantage. For the first several kilometres he fell with almost every step, until he finally mastered the distinctive gait necessary to take advantage of the ungainly apparatus.

Hours later he'd made so little progress and was so discouraged that he thought briefly of heading back to the security of the work camp—boring or not. The knowledge of the unrelenting teasing that he knew he'd take was the only thing that made Fred press on. Even the thought of finding the seemingly mythical miner had little importance to him now.

At ten that night, a bone-weary Fred turned off the trail in search of a trappers' cabin that he'd heard was nearby. He did find it, but many weeks too late to do him any good. The makeshift shelter had collapsed under the weight of the snow on its roof. He chose a spruce tree as shelter instead and pulled some of the food that he'd brought out of his pack.

Refreshed by the nourishment, Fred headed out again, this time in a more positive frame of mind. He *would* make it, he told himself, as long as he kept going. Although it had been dark for some time, the snow reflected the light of the moon and the stars and provided enough illumination to allow him to see his way. As midnight approached, though, the night suddenly became darker. Fred looked up and realized that clouds were scuttling across the sky. Moments later, and oddly, since it was early February, it began to rain. The optimistic mood of little more than hour before gave way to near-panic.

It was too dark now for Fred to see his way and soon he was soaking wet. Worse, he was walking on several metres of snow that was rapidly turning to slush with the rain pelting down on it. He couldn't think of stopping—he knew that if he did stop he'd eventually freeze to death, particularly if the temperature dropped—but keeping going was nearly impossible. He inched his way along, fighting to remain conscious, as the cold penetrated his bones and hypothermia began to set in.

Just when Fred was sure that his situation could not get worse, it did. A strong northerly wind whipped up. Anything with any moisture in it, including Fred's clothing, quickly became coated in a layer of ice. He willed himself to keep going by focusing on the concept that to stop now would mean certain death. Just a few steps more and the weakened man was driven to his knees by the gusts of freezing rain and the weight of the ice that encrusted him. The once-confident and foolhardy young man pushed on as long as he was able. He was within sight of the Monashee Range when his will to carry on finally gave out.

Telling himself that he'd only rest for a moment or two, he dragged himself to the base of a huge sheltering tree. Even though he knew that staying there for just a few minutes would unquestionably mean death, he was unable to resist the temptation. Embracing the opportunity to lose consciousness, Fred was drifting away when an unseen force jolted him awake. He jumped to his feet and scanned what he was able to see of the horizon around him. The storm's strength was continuing to build. Totally disoriented, the frozen and half-dead man had no idea in which direction safety lay. He stood for only a second before deciding that lying down to die right where he was would be his most sensible choice.

Then, just in front of him, Fred thought that he saw something vaguely human-shaped approaching through the blowing maelstrom. It couldn't be! He must be hallucinating, he told himself. Still, though, it really did look like the outline of a man. A man in a hooded robe stood not 15 metres (50 feet) from Fred and was signalling for Fred to follow him. Unsure at first as to what he was seeing and how best to respond, Fred merely stood and stared. He suddenly realized that the gesturing manifestation in front of him looked familiar. It was the vision that had appeared in the water glass at the bunk-house that November night. That apparition had been a precursor to the appearance in the storm. Now Fred understood why the ghost of his friend had seemed so angry that night as he looked into (as he now realized) the future: Jack's spirit had to leave its eternal rest in order to guide Fred out of the danger that he'd foolishly placed himself in.

Barely conscious, Fred followed the phantom, even though the image was heading in exactly the opposite direction from that which Fred's badly muddled mind told him safety lay in. Faster and faster the two went, the phantom always staying just beyond Fred's reach. With each step, Fred became warmer and more lucid. He determined that the smoothness with which his former friend moved across the ice-coated, snowy terrain meant that the other man must have the advantage of gliding along on skis.

At the bottom of a slope, and protected from the wind, Fred finally began to feel that he was back in the land of the living. He looked around and spotted a cabin just ahead. As he headed to the shelter, Fred turned to call out a thank you to his phantom friend, but Black Jack McFarlane was nowhere to be seen.

The door to the refuge was unlocked and Fred Lindsay let himself in. Seconds later, he was collapsed beneath a pile of blankets on a bed in the corner of the rough-hewn little log dwelling. He slept the clock around without waking. When he finally did come awake, Fred helped himself to the provisions that he found on the cabin's shelves. As soon as he was able, he looked outside. The turbulent weather had died down, and no more snow or rain had fallen while he'd been sleeping.

Hesitantly, Fred made his way out the door. His own snowshoe prints were clearly visible where he had come down the hill and into the cabin, but nowhere was there any sign that his friend Black Jack had also made the trek. There were no footprints, snowshoe tracks or grooves from skis. It was as if the image that Fred had seen so clearly had either not been there, or had been gliding just above the snow.

His body rested and fed and his curiosity provoked, Fred

retraced his tracks up the hillside until he came to the tree that he'd collapsed under. It had been easy to find again, for his snowshoe markings led him directly there. He was shocked to realize that the ghost had not only led him to safety, but also away from certain death. If Fred had followed his own inclinations, he would have fallen over a sheer cliff into a crevice and hit the granite boulders more than 100 metres (300 feet) below.

It took two visits from the ghost of his friend Jack McFarlane to shake Fred Lindsay's scepticism, but from that day onward the man believed in spirits. From this new perspective, he looked back at the events of his past, including a life-threatening incident in his younger days.

At the time, he was working as a brakeman on a logging train on Vancouver Island. He had been riding on a car full of logs as the engineer rounded a bend too quickly. The rolling stock buckled at Fred's car, derailing that car and causing it to rip up track in its path. Something or someone had plucked the youth from his perch and

When you're nearly dead from hypothermia, even a rustic cabin like this one is a sight for sore eyes.

placed him on a ledge 5 metres (16 feet) over from where he'd been and 4 metres (13 feet) higher.

As he clung to his precarious hold, Fred watched the action unfold below him. After the train stopped, he noted that none of his fellow crew members had apparently been injured either, for they were all running about shouting his name. When he was composed enough to respond, Fred called out to them to assure them he was alive. He then cautiously made his way down the embankment to the accident site below. There, one of his coworkers told him how he'd seen Fred appear to fly up and away from danger, as if propelled by some invisible hand.

At the time Fred hadn't known who or what had been responsible for his inexplicable escape from death. It wasn't until his second brush with the Grim Reaper that the man finally accepted the reality of forces from beyond our realm.

By the way, this ghost story ends on a further positive note. Fred Lindsay did find the miner whom he'd risked his life to search for and he did become the man's partner. And, as long as he lived, he never forgot his supernatural life-saver.

Chapter 9

A POTPOURRI OF PRESENCES

Although it is always most gratifying to find a true ghost story completely intact, we must often settle for mere fragments of tales. Some of the following stories are examples of instances where the details of a haunting may have been lost to history.

Readers occasionally tell me that they find this incompleteness frustrating, but I've come to appreciate these "spirit snippets" for their longevity. A few of the following anecdotes have been passed along from person to person so many times that they have become twice-told tales or urban legends. Some of the accounts in this section are not truly ghost stories, since they deal with "angelic interventions." No matter what you call them, I hope that you will find all of these paranormal stories both engaging and entertaining.

It has become apparent to me that some people are very much more likely to see a ghost than are others. Those who tend toward sightings simply seem to be more perceptive of the spirit world—in effect, more "tuned to the wavelength," if you will, of the ethereal realm. As a result, some people take ghost sightings as a natural part of their day-to-day lives, whereas others will go to their graves never having seen or even felt the presence of a ghost.

If some people are more likely to be treated to a glimpse of the world beyond, is the reverse also true? That is, are some spirits more likely than others to appear in our everyday world? Based on a review of the documentation available, it would appear that the stronger a person's personality was in life, the greater the chance of that person's ghost visiting the living. This concept is especially interesting when you consider that, over the years and all around the world, the most frequently seen apparitions are ones connected with Christianity.

The Virgin Mary is the image that people see most frequently. Such sightings have been reported from all over the world, including here in Canada. A more unusual manifestation, however, occurred in the southern Vancouver Island town of Ladysmith in the summer of 1986.

Images began appearing on the living-room wall of an otherwise unremarkable townhouse. The little girl who first noticed the markings announced, "a man is coming through the wall." According to the people who lived there, "a dark outline on a plaster wall" appeared to be "the smudged features of Jesus Christ, with a cross over his forehead."

Once word of the oddity got out, the residents began receiving visitors from all over the world. Some of them said that they could feel heat radiating from the shapes on the wall. As word spread, the number of images began to increase. The face of a recently deceased foster daughter became visible, followed by "a curly headed bearded man" whose identity was something of a riddle. Some witnesses claimed that the second man was one of Christ's disciples, but the man living in the house claimed that the man depicted bore a striking resemblance to his brother, who had died just before his foster daughter had.

Though the growing number of faces visible on the wall was remarkable in itself, one of the images that formed was more startling than the others: it showed a man with a rope around his neck.

Not long after the strange appearances began, the townhouse was sold; I do not know what happened to the images.

Angel sightings and interventions could be said to fall midway between religious and paranormal experiences. With the increasing popularity of the idea that angels are among us over the last ten years of the twentieth century, the belief in such supernatural beings has now become mainstream. The following three personal tales of angels assisting mortals were reported on in the *Calgary Herald* on Christmas Eve 1992.

Bob McKenzie was a young man, barely out of his teens, when the following encounter took place. In 1972, he and two friends were in the tony Shaughnessy area of Vancouver. At the intersection of Granville Street and King Edward Avenue they noticed a couple of teenage boys who appeared to be up to no good. Bob decided to give the youngsters a scare, as well as perhaps also prevent a crime from being committed. With great bluff and bravado, he approached the teens in a manner that he hoped would lead them to the erroneous conclusion that he was an undercover police officer.

McKenzie spoke sternly to the lads, asking to see some identification. The younger men were immediately intimidated and showed every sign of moving on at the first possible opportunity—until they heard laughter coming from the car that Bob had just gotten out of. The youngsters quickly realized that these men were not officers at all, merely some fellows pulling their own prank. Not only did this realization re-establish the youths' courage, but seconds later they were joined by more than a dozen of their friends. Now the tables were turned.

With fifteen "of the meanest-looking hoods" that he'd ever seen bearing down on him, Bob McKenzie was petrified with fear. As he stood there helplessly, the gang closed in on him. When his attackers were only 1 metre (3 feet) from where he stood, Bob reported that they suddenly stopped, "as if they [had] hit a shield."

Bob took advantage of his enemies' apparent paralysis and immediately dove into the safety of his friend's car. He slammed and locked the car door but, before the driver had a chance to accelerate away, the invisible fortification that had held the youths back dissolved. The gang charged *en masse* toward the side of the car, reaching its parking place just as the three frightened young men sped to safety.

The incident confirmed Bob McKenzie's pre-existing belief in angels—and hopefully it also deterred him from ever again playing such a dangerous practical joke.

A young woman named Dawn had been suffering terribly as a result of a tragic freak accident that had killed her sister, Melody. While on a trip to Valemount, near the Alberta border in east-central British Columbia, Melody had fallen over the edge of a cliff and had drowned in the water below. She'd been wearing an outfit of Dawn's at the time. As Melody was shorter than Dawn, the pant legs would have been too long for the smaller girl and Dawn had always wondered since then if tripping on them had possibly caused her sister's fatal tumble.

One morning in 1977, three years after the accident, Dawn was standing in her kitchen chatting with friends. She was facing the door to an unused bedroom, one that was always kept closed. Today, however, the door stood open; it struck Dawn as being so strange that she mentioned it to her friends. As she moved toward the door to close it, an illuminated corridor appeared. Melody stood at the end of it, smiling happily at her. For the first time since her sister's death, Dawn felt at peace.

That incident not only relieved Dawn's feelings of guilt in connection with her sister's death, but it let her know that Melody was happy where she was. Since that first visitation, Dawn has continued to sense Melody's spirit with her and has come to count on the comfort and support of a very special guardian angel.

In the 1970s, John of Vancouver, whose last name has been withheld to protect his privacy, had finally had enough of the drug scene. Unfortunately, by the time that he made this decision, he had also become thoroughly addicted, at least psychologically, to LSD.

Thinking that there was no hope for him, John prepared to take his own life. He stood on the railing of the Granville Street Bridge, intending to hurl himself into the water below. As he composed himself before jumping to his death, John felt a hand grab his arm. He was certain that an alert police officer had spotted him and rushed to foil his suicide attempt.

John turned to push his saviour aside. The person holding onto him, however, was not from this realm and it was certainly not a police officer. "It was Jesus," the distressed man concluded.

The image communicated to John without speaking, directed him to go home and then vanished before the man's eyes. To this day, John debates whether the encounter was a product of his drug-addled mind or whether he actually experienced divine intervention. Perhaps such answers are not that important and all that really matters is that John did not kill himself, and then went on to recover from drug dependency.

Many reports of near-death experiences seem similar to angelic interventions.

A British Columbia resident whom we'll identify only as "June H." was travelling home from the funeral for her stepfather, George. She was a passenger and her friend Clarence was the driver. As they made their way from the cemetery, they were involved in a dreadful collision.

June was seriously injured but did eventually recover from her injuries. During her recovery she recalled that, at the moment of impact between the two vehicles, George had appeared to her in a foggy cloud. He had touched her and told her to "go back" and had explained that it was "not time yet" for her to join him.

Clarence, however, had not been so fortunate: he had died at the scene of the accident. Judging by June's experiences for a number of weeks after the accident, poor Clarence was dissatisfied to find that June was no longer with him. The first time that his image appeared to June, she had been asleep in bed. She awoke to see her dead friend in the room with her, holding out his hand to her and beckoning her to join him.

Startled, June immediately turned on the light beside her bed. The image vanished. But, as soon as she turned the light off, it was there again. The man must really have been desperate to have June with him, for he reappeared over the next few days, gaining strength with each visit. On subsequent visits, he pulled June's bed-covers off her and once even tried to pick her up.

June resorted to sleeping with the light on. Eventually Clarence's energy dissipated and she no longer saw or felt her former friend.

Urban legends, modern myths—we're fascinated by them. It is intriguing that new ones are continually being introduced into the mix and older ones are apparently revised to keep up with society's changes. For our purposes, though, the very best tales are built around ghosts.

A staple subject of the urban legend repertoire is the vanishing hitchhiker—an apparition that suddenly appears at the side of a road, often seemingly in need of assistance. Such a recurring ghost story is played out on University Boulevard, which leads to the University of British Columbia on the west side of Vancouver. It is said that the vision of a woman haunts that particular strip of road because that is where she was hitchhiking when she was picked up by a young man. Perhaps to impress the girl, he began driving recklessly. He soon lost control of the car and slammed it into a tree. Both of them were killed instantly.

Drivers in that vicinity have spoken of seeing a young woman thumbing a lift at the side of the road. Some said that they pulled their cars over to the side of the road near her image, only to find that she had vanished into thin air. Others indicated that she got into their car and actually spoke to the driver, advising him or her of the address that she wanted to go to. In each case they then proceeded directly to that address but, when they reached the destination, the driver was shocked to realize that he or she was completely alone in the car. The hitchhiker had vanished.

Four young men, driving at night near the campus, reported the following encounter, which has a somewhat different twist. The weather was bad and they were surprised to see a young woman dressed in white hitchhiking at the side of the road. They stopped and let her into their car. She gave them an address, but, as they passed through the University Endowment Lands, their female passenger vanished. Badly unnerved, the men decided to proceed to the address that the apparition had mentioned. Once there, they knocked on the door and explained what had happened. The man who answered their knock told them that they were not the first to come to him with such a tale and that his daughter had been the victim of a hit-and-run accident near the University of British Columbia campus on a stormy night some years before.

An even stranger anomaly exists just east of Horseshoe Bay, near Cypress Creek. A taxi driver swore that he saw a ghost at the side of the Upper Levels Highway. As he told others of his strange encounter, he began hearing other, equally odd, descriptions from a few of the drivers who'd taken that route. Most commonly, they spoke of their car moving as though it were controlled by "an inexplicable force."

Highway workers in the area contend that the sightings and sensations result from drivers becoming somewhat mesmerized while travelling along the curvy mountainside highway surrounded by beautiful scenery. Although these factors may have an effect, it is also interesting to note that the history of the area's Native people indicates that that particular tract of land was once the site of a vicious battle between the Haida and the Squamish peoples. Perhaps that battle has somehow permanently scarred the area's psychic atmosphere.

The pitiful-looking "Lady in Black" appears at the side of East Sooke Road in East Sooke, west of Victoria. This tale is somewhat unusual as the people in the community are fairly certain that they know the ghost's identity. The phantom is probably the spirit of Louisa May Stiff, a former school teacher in the area. All who see her report that poor Louisa is apparently eternally still and forlorn. Her face is starkly white, making an eerie contrast to the old-fashioned black dress she is wearing.

Not far from East Sooke, at a place once known as "China Flats" (roughly halfway between Sooke and Victoria), the ghost of a man is sometimes seen at the side of the road. He has reportedly lunged out in front of cars in order to try to make the drivers stop.

This particular phantom hitchhiker is such a common sighting that, when his ghost was mentioned on a radio show, the station's lines were jammed with calls. Dozens of people wanted to share their experiences on that eerie section of the highway. Not everyone had actually seen the apparition. Some reported being overcome by a sudden and unexplainable feeling that they were not alone in the car.

A sad piece of local history is enough to explain why that area is haunted. In the 1940s, a woman living in the area with her husband became seriously ill. The man knew that he had to get medical help soon or it would be too late. As they didn't have a car, he ran to the road and tried in vain to flag down passing motorists. When no one would even slow down, the worried husband stood in the middle of the road waving his arms at an oncoming car. The driver either did not see the man signalling or saw him too late to either swerve or stop. The distraught man was hit by the car and died instantly.

When the police who investigated the accident went to report the death to the man's widow, they found that she too had died. Evidently, the man's spirit has not yet been able to accept that he will forever be unable to save either his wife or himself.

"Dancing Mary" has also been seen to manifest on a Vancouver Island roadway. Local history indicates that this wraith has made her ghostly appearances at the side of the road near Comox. She was a young woman, a bride-to-be, when she disappeared. The townsfolk presumed that, in one of his drunken rages, her fiancé had beaten her to death. The first sighting occurred not long afterward. An area farmer was riding his bicycle up Comox Hill Road when he spied an illuminated blue mist on the road ahead. A closer look revealed a figure inside the mist—a figure of a young woman, dancing.

In the 1940s, a soldier stationed in the town was returning to his base, also by bicycle. As he made his way along the road, he was most surprised to see a strange, and very localized, blue fog almost right in front of him. The unusual sighting startled him but, when he looked more closely and saw a lone woman dancing enveloped in the fog, he became frightened. When she extended her arm toward him, beckoning the soldier to join her, he fled past the enigma in terror. As he rode through the spot where the image had been, he became chilled to the bone. At the other side of that spot the air returned to its normal temperature.

In 1986, three teenaged boys took the kind of bike trip that they'll remember for the rest of their lives. The main event of this story occurred to the northeast of Sooke—specifically on Sooke Lake Road, not far from the Island Highway. Phyllis Griffiths, the mother of two of the lads involved, described "a grey and foggy mid-October afternoon" when the "boys decided to go on a bicycling trip to Goldstream Provincial Park."

According to what they reported when they returned home much later that day, the boys—Ken and Chris Griffiths and their friend, Mike Waring—enjoyed their day of exploration. The only components of the trip that they considered a bit out of the ordinary were the thick pockets of fog that they had encountered while pedalling along Sooke Lake Road. Other than that, there was little remarkable, they thought, on which to report.

One of the boys, however, did think to mention a building that they'd seen. Phyllis was most interested in his description of the building, for it was at a place that she knew well. Oddly, the boy indicated that it was a large, ornate building. However, the building that Phyllis knew to be at the location that she had in mind, Ma Miller's Pub, was not as big as he was describing. The two looked at one another in puzzlement before proceeding to try to clear up the confusion. Perhaps determining exactly where the building stood would help. Unfortunately, this approach actually succeeded in complicating the discussion further: although Phyllis insisted that the place was on one side of the road, the boys had seen a building on the opposite side.

No doubt feeling extremely dissatisfied with the way that the discussion had gone, the little group dispersed. They might never have mentioned the strange misunderstanding again had Phyllis Griffiths not been a volunteer at the Goldstream Region Museum. When she was at work, shortly after her strange conversation with the boys, she thought to pull the museum's file about the building in question. In that file she found the answer to the disagreement.

That answer, however, created an entire series of new and provocative questions.

The archival records indicated that Ma Miller's Pub, at the corner of Sooke Lake Road and Humpback Road, had once been called the Goldstream Inn. In earlier days, the inn had been a much larger and more ornate structure than the current one and it had indeed been located across the road from the current building.

Phyllis Griffiths showed an old photograph of the original inn to one of her sons. She reported that "he went white" when he realized that the building that he and his companions had seen on that fall afternoon had not physically existed since the 1920s.

Some people believe that a link exists between ghostly sightings and humidity. This story certainly supports such a theory: the Goldstream Inn, a place that no longer exists, had appeared out of a fog to give three teenaged boys an adventure with an unexpected ghostly twist—even though they didn't know it at the time.

In the late 1800s and early 1900s, roughly between Spences Bridge and Ashcroft, near what would become Highway 1, there existed a small, isolated Chinese community. As the children of those settlers moved on, the barely adequate roadside housing was simply left to tumble down until the lumber and other building materials eventually decayed into the ground. In 1975 the ruins of the little settlement were still visible, as was the frightening-looking ghost of one of the former inhabitants.

Despite appearing in a very solid form, anyone who saw this apparition knew immediately that what they were observing was not human. Though the entity was clearly female and clearly of Asian descent, it was also clearly from another time and dimension.

Because she has always been seen walking along the side of the road by herself late at night, motorists have inevitably stopped to ask if she needs assistance. From all reports, those good Samaritans didn't stop for long. One close look at her almost-iridescent skin, sneering mouth and dark, piercing eyes quickly convinced the well-meaning folks that it would be best to move along out of this strange entity's reach.

An intriguing story ran in the *Vancouver Sun* on March 15, 1950. It described a novel called *Judith*, which had been written by Blanche Draper of Robson Street in Vancouver and published by Christopher Publishing House of Boston earlier that year.

The article went on to anticipate any questions that readers might have of author Draper's credibility by asserting that not only was she the daughter of an Anglican minister but also that she had been "educated under the strict supervision of Anglican ethics."

Under normal conditions, these protestations might not have been necessary but, considering the unusual circumstances under which this book was created, they seemed warranted. Blanche Draper staunchly maintained that she had been only an "instrument" in the writing of the novel and that every word of it had been dictated to her by the ghost of English author Marie Corelli, who had died in 1924.

"I could not see Marie Corelli nor hear her voice [but] she did the writing. I was the instrument. The pencil simply flew." The script that that pencil produced as it "flew," Draper noted, was very different in appearance from her own penmanship.

Draper's and Corelli's British Columbia-based collaboration bore a striking resemblance to a world-famous automatism case that had its inception during the summer of 1913.

Using a Ouija board, a St. Louis, Missouri, homemaker named Pearl Curran made contact with the spirit of Patience Worth. The entity explained that she had grown up as an English peasant in the mid-1600s. Apparently, her soul's time and place of incarnation in this earthly realm had prevented Patience from enjoying either reading or writing; she wanted, through Curran, to change that.

Over the next ten years, Curran claimed that Worth's spirit had dictated, initially through the Ouija board and later via automatic speech, books of poetry, short stories, plays and six historical novels. Worth's supernatural body of work became extremely popular and scholars who examined the writing attested to its historical detail and accuracy, as well as its literary merit.

It is difficult to say whether the results of the British Columbia-based automatism case might have been equally impressive in terms of literary talent and historical detail, because a thorough search through the records of *Books in Print* did not turn up any such book. There are no listings at all for an author named "Blanche A. Draper." Marie Corelli, however, is well represented. An astounding thirty-four of her titles are still in print, but none are entitled *Judith* and none were published in 1950. Whatever happened to the Draper-Corelli collaboration written about on the Ides of March 1950 by an unnamed newspaper scribe, remains a mystery.

On a moonless night in 1942, a railway worker in the Canadian Pacific Railway train yards at the north foot of Vancouver's Granville Street caught what might have been the last glimpse of a legendary spectre that had been haunting the place for over a dozen years.

The phantom sightings may have ended that night, but the ghost story of Hub Clark has lived on as a classic British Columbia tale. It seems that on an unpleasantly wet night in 1928, brakeman Clark slipped as he jumped from a train in the train yards. His head slammed on a rail belonging to a parallel track and he was knocked unconscious. Moments later, a train was shunted down that track and Hub Clark was decapitated.

Reports of a headless apparition began on the next stormy night. The entity was generally presumed to be the ghost of Hub Clark trying to warn others about the danger of the rain-slicked surfaces. Because his image has not been seen for nearly sixty years, it is presumed that the soul of the ill-fated brakeman has now gone on to his eternal rest.

The building housing Mushroom Studios on West 6th Avenue is another haunted spot in Vancouver. It seems reasonable to assume that the ghost was either a musician or, at the very least, someone who appreciated music, because the phantom can be heard humming or singing along during recording sessions. The entity doesn't restrict itself to accompaniment, though. It has been known to put on something of a solo vocal act through the studio's monitors when they are not already in use by living performers.

According to a 1924 newspaper article, "Jumping Rock" was a well-known landmark close to shipping routes near where British Columbia gives way to the Alaska Panhandle. This "high and ugly promontory" was described as jutting out into "the bleak north Pacific."

Two young Natives who lived near this landmark were heartbroken that their parents would not allow them to marry one another. They were deeply in love, but both had been promised in marriage to members of other tribes. They could see no point in living if they couldn't be together and so they planned to kill themselves by jumping from the huge rock to a sure death by drowning. As they stood poised for their double suicide, the would-be bride apparently changed her mind at the last minute and her beloved went to his death alone.

Ever since that incident, sailors have avoided travelling through the waters directly below Jumping Rock. They say that the area is haunted by the angry ghost of a young brave.

Here are two examples of how only the most basic details of ghostly tales have as yet found their way to me (though I am always open to hearing from someone who possesses additional information): In the late 1970s, a ghost haunted a hairdressing salon located on No. 3 Road in Richmond. Across Georgia Strait, another, more vengeful spirit once crashed a Tupperware party on Raynor Avenue in Victoria. The guests left without their refrigerator containers.

In the March 10, 1995, edition of *Entertainment Weekly*, Gillian Anderson, the actress who plays Dana Scully on *X-Files*, the enormously popular television show about various aspects of the paranormal, is quoted as saying that the Lower Mainland house that she and her husband lived in had been haunted. "It was creepy," Anderson acknowledged of the house, which was located near a Native burial ground. "It felt like there was someone attached to me."

The couple arranged for a smudging ceremony to cleanse the house. The ritual was evidently sufficient and successful as she added that she felt the spirits had, by the time the *Entertainment Weekly* interview took place, departed.

It is unlikely that the haunted cabin of the following story still exists. It no doubt tumbled down and rotted into the soil that it was built on many, many years ago. However, the disappearance of the cabin does not necessarily mean that the ghost has left the area—especially not this ghost, for he seemed a most determined soul.

The year was 1898 and Dan O'Ryan, like countless thousands of others, was anxious to make his fortune by joining the rush for gold. Unlike most of those who trekked along with him, Dan really did strike it rich. He was heading back down the British Columbia coast with his treasure when he stopped to rest for the night in an abandoned cabin. In order to protect his gold, Dan dug a series of deep trenches and buried his treasure. Then, filled with ill-placed trust, Dan made himself at home in the tiny building and immediately went to sleep for the night.

Dan O'Ryan never woke up again. Other fortune hunters, those who had not been as fortunate as he, had followed him. They murdered the sleeping man and stole as much of his gold as they could find before slinking away into the night.

The thieving murderers were never caught and Dan O'Ryan's desperate soul has never rested since. Travellers along the isolated route reported seeing smoke coming from the chimney of that abandoned, ramshackle cabin. And, on the surrounding land, they say, an image can be seen of a man frantically digging. Digging as though for something valuable that he buried but now is unable to find.

In the 1920s, Francis Rattenbury designed many of the spectacular buildings in the capital city, Victoria. For a few years the man was very much the toast of the town. His fortunes, however, were to fail him. The man who once dominated the social and professional scene in Victoria fled for England after being ostracized by his peers as a result of an indiscreet affair and subsequent marriage.

Since he was murdered by his new wife's lover, he might have led a happier and longer life if he'd stopped to listen to those who thought he was acting foolishly. Given his fall from grace after such magnificent architectural accomplishments, it isn't surprising to think that his soul has sought solace in the halls of his masterpiece—

the Parliament Buildings—where some people say that his spirit continues to roam the halls to this day.

A report in a Calgary newspaper supplement told of a most dramatic haunting in Victoria. The journalist who compiled the special Hallowe'en article did not pinpoint the exact location, but referred to it only as "the malevolent House on the Hill." He described dinner napkins that spontaneously burst into flames, "furniture [that] moved and dark forces [that] prowled the rooms and grounds."

Although it wasn't alluded to in that particular piece, such a haunting would have been the work of a poltergeist, an active spirit who is usually associated with a person rather than a place. It would probably be a safe bet that there was a child, near or in adolescence, in that "House on the Hill" during the time of those paranormal activities.

Architect Francis Rattenbury may still roam the halls of the Parliament Buildings in Victoria.

Many years ago, a trapper in northern British Columbia found himself down on his luck. His wife and children left him and the man was doomed to live out his days in his isolated cabin with only his faithful dog for companionship.

Not many months later, the man was so forlorn that he realized he could not go on living. After leaving his dog in the care of an acquaintance, the man made his way to the coast and threw himself from a rocky ledge into the ocean below. According to a newspaper report of the day, "He left a note fastened to a jackpine nearby, explaining that he was tired of living."

The authorities carried out a cursory search, but, when his body was not found within a short time, the investigation was called off. It was presumed that the distraught man's body had simply become fish food. They so advised the man's estranged next of kin.

Eventually, the story of the suicide got back to the man who'd been left with the deceased's dog—and he had an interesting tale of his own to tell. It seems that the day after the dog's owner had abandoned him, the animal began acting strangely, running to the edge of the property and barking madly. This activity went on for some days and each time the agitated dog moved farther and farther away from his temporary home. A few weeks later, he disappeared altogether. The man who'd been left responsible for the dog was troubled by the disappearance and, whenever he went out anywhere, he made a point of looking for the lost animal.

Three weeks after the dog ran off, when the man was walking along the rocky coast, he met some people who'd been camped there for some time and it was then that he learned the fate of the missing dog. The campers told of a dog that matched the description of the one he asked about and said that it had shown up one night near their campsite.

They recalled that the dog had "displayed great uneasiness, whining and scampering up and down ... several times crouching as though about to spring into the water." Because the witnesses to the animal's bizarre behaviour knew nothing of its owner's suicide, they "were at a loss to account for the animal's actions."

Not knowing what else they could do, the party merely watched the animal. When a storm came up, however, they were worried for its safety and tried to coax the dog to come away from the ledge and take shelter with them. The determined canine would have none of it. Even when he was offered food, he would not leave his post near the water, nor would he stop barking and pacing back and forth.

"He sees something," the campers finally realized as they too looked into the choppy waters below.

Then, as the people stared, an arm broke the surface of the waves. "It seemed to beckon and the dog, with one final joyous yelp, leaped into the [water] and dropped from sight," they reported.

Revealing their understanding of the sort of behaviour that one might normally expect from a dog, they added, "Another dog might have struck out at once and commenced to swim, but this one didn't. He had gone to join his old master."

The writer reporting this story closed with the assurance that "the witnesses, who were entirely sober, have gone on oath about the waving arm."

Amid a grove of poplars on a tiny island off the coast of northern British Columbia there was, and may still be, a small cabin. For years, tired anglers and boaters were grateful to come across this temporary shelter—until the little place became haunted by an entity with some frightening behaviours.

Women especially have reported that their sleep in the cabin has been disturbed by an unnerving paranormal force. One woman, who'd travelled north from Victoria, "awoke in the dead of night to find a ghostly hand on [her] shoulder and ghostly breath fanning [her] cheek." Although those sensations were distressing enough, the experience merely set her nerves on edge in preparation for subsequent ghostly sounds. She later heard "moaning and screaming." Not surprisingly, the woman was terrified and fled at once.

Another woman awoke to find her neck scratched from ear to ear. Others who have tried to sleep in the haunted cabin maintain that, after they feel the phantom's hand on their shoulder, there are finger marks on their skin. Although no one has ever seen the ghost, there's not much question as to its existence.

On another island sits an abandoned salmon cannery that is said to be haunted. Two men and a woman who were employed at the cannery were involved in a love triangle. One evening, when the woman and one of her boyfriends were walking on the beach, they were attacked "by two powerful men, bound and carried down to one of the fishboats and taken out to the open sea."

Neither was ever seen alive again. Shortly after their disappearance, the second man gave up his job at the cannery and left the area for good. It was said by those still who remained working at the cannery that the ghost of the woman came "back to revisit the scene, searching perhaps for her old lover." Many workers at the cannery came "face to face with her in the dusky corners of the packing shed." There is no question as to whose spirit it was that they saw, for her image was always clad in "the same yellow shawl [that] she wore in life."

Just weeks after the Fathers of Confederation made headlines with the creation of the Dominion of Canada, a ghost story was making its own headlines in the Cariboo Country of what would one day be British Columbia. It seems that miners working at

Mosquito Gulch near Barkerville were frightened to enter the mine tunnels for fear of encountering a ghost. Up until that difficulty arose, the Minnehaha Company had been successfully mining lead on its claim. Then its employees began to report seeing a ghost of "hideous appearance" in the mine. The miners' fears were so great that they effectively shut down the mining operation.

Not wanting to abandon a lucrative seam, the company called in spiritualists and various respected members of the community to exorcise the mine tunnels. A party of seventeen men assembled at Jeffree's store before heading *en masse* to the haunted mine. After the spiritualists performed the rites of exorcism outside the entrance to the main shaft, the group waited, hoping to witness something that would indicate that the spirit had been driven from the mine.

When, according to an article in the *Cariboo Sentinel* on September 23, 1867, "no ghost appeared," the committee chose three of their number to go down into the tunnel and confront the ghost directly. The trio "reported that after careful search they could find no ghost in the Minnehaha diggings." It is reasonable to believe then, that the exorcism had actually been a success. Despite this assurance, the mining company had difficulty convincing miners to return to the shafts. With much regret, the company began to search for lead deposits elsewhere. A paranormal presence—a ghost—had forced them to abandon a profitable business venture.

People come from all over the world to ski the fabulous slopes at Whistler, which is about two hours' drive north of Vancouver. At least three of these folks have never left. A ghostly presence is said to roam the halls at the Whistler Creek Lodge and there are two of the happiest ghosts ever reported in the adjacent restaurant. The pair, thought to be a mother and her twelve-year-old daughter, sit up in the dining-room's rafters and laugh as though they're seeing something uproariously funny.

Very near the comfortably contemporary Hillside Shopping Centre in Victoria hides an out-of-date scene that makes those who witness it most *un*comfortable. On Shelbourne Street, near this shopping mall, people have reported coming upon an especially eerie scene, a scene from the past.

These retrocognitive sightings have all been remarkably similar and occurred under equally remarkably similar circumstances. The "peek into the past" most commonly comes in the month of October, during the wee hours of a Sunday morning. Drivers who've up until then noticed nothing out of the ordinary will slam on their brakes and bring their cars to a screeching halt after suddenly having entered a scene right out of the past.

They are shocked to discover that the paved roads, modern buildings, light standards and billboards that they'd taken for granted in that area have disappeared. Worse, those familiar surroundings have been replaced by a meandering, overgrown country road, with untended grass and weeds grow up tall between the ruts in the dirt and bulrushes growing in the marshy ditches where the sidewalks should be. The road is now completely unlit except by any moonlight that might be present.

Inevitably, the people who become entangled in this time shift are immediately disoriented and, understandably, in a state approaching panic. They say that in the time that it takes them to calm down sufficiently to create a coherent thought—one that usually involves finding a spot to turn their car around—the country road from the past disappears and they are once again staring out into their familiar, contemporary environment.

Take note, though, if you're thinking that it would be great fun to gather a group of friends on a Sunday morning in October and drive around near Victoria's Hillside Shopping Centre during the hours from midnight to dawn to see if you can time-travel together. There's no point in taking anyone with you if you want to experience this phenomenon. Perhaps you should reconsider your plan and reassess your level of courage, because this spooky scene has only been known to appear to drivers who are alone in their cars.

Chapter 10

PARANORMAL BRITISH COLUMBIA

Beautiful British Columbia's supernatural qualities extend well beyond the effective tourism industry marketing slogan. And ghosts are not the only paranormal phenomena associated with the province. In addition to an entire population of West Coast spectres, British Columbia apparently hosts mysterious creatures in its waters and forests—and even in the skies overhead. Monsters, either on land or in the water, and unidentified flying objects make for tales that are very different from ghost stories but, I hope you will agree, equally intriguing and entertaining.

The Sasquatch

Starting at the beginning has always seemed to me to be a logical approach. Therefore I naïvely began to scan archived newspapers for the first public acknowledgement of the creature that Canadians refer to as "sasquatch" and Americans know as "bigfoot." It was several weeks before I finally realized that what I sought would be found within a totally different medium. The first recognition of the beast's existence was not in typeset words, but in carved images—renderings chiselled into the wooden totem poles of the First Nations peoples of northwestern North America.

The large and elusive sasquatch was not just a mysterious legend to these people: it was a dangerous reality. Its inclusion on totem poles was intended to both recognize the existence of the species and warn of the threat that it represented.

When non-Natives began exploring the "New World," First Nations people advised them of the frightening beasts in the woods. As explorer David Thompson's expedition made its way across the Rocky Mountains, into what is now British Columbia, Natives that Thompson encountered told him about a huge, hairy creature and warned him of its dangers. Thompson recorded those cautions in his journal on January 5, 1811. On January 7, his diary entry records his party as having found the enormous footprints of a biped frozen into the terrain along their exploration route. This discovery immediately changed Thompson's somewhat amused scepticism to fearful respect for the creature that had created those humbling prints.

A First Nations group living along the West Coast recalled times when some of their people had returned from fishing and hunting trips with terrifying stories about "giants" standing on the banks of rivers bombarding them with huge stones, and about being chased through the woods by the "susquash."

Even American President Theodore Roosevelt acknowledged the beast's existence in his book *Wilderness Hunter*. He included a long narrative about the experiences of two hunters who, after finding huge tracks, tried to stalk the animal, but found that it was stalking them instead. The contest of hunting skills ended when one of the hunters fled after finding his partner's body. The deceased's neck had been snapped and his throat sliced open. The survivor described the lethal wounds as looking like they had been caused by four huge claws.

One of the most amazing encounters with this creature occurred in southwestern British Columbia at the beginning of July in 1884. The crew on a train travelling between Lytton and Yale alongside the Thompson River spotted a strange creature not far from the tracks. As the engineer applied the brakes, several men on board jumped from the train and pursued—and actually caught—the gorilla-like beast. They caged the hairy oddity, which they named "Jacko." It was determined by his height—140 centimetres (4 feet, 7 inches)—and weight—57.6 kilograms (127 pounds)—that Jacko was a youngster.

No one knows what eventually happened to this diminutive sasquatch. There had been talk of transporting him to England for exhibition and it is commonly accepted that the captured animal succumbed to the combined torments of incarceration and transportation. The story, however, remains a classic in sasquatch lore.

Although sightings continued throughout the province, no further specimens were ever captured. In 1924, however, quite the reverse is said to have occurred. Alfred Ostman, who was searching for a lost gold mine in the Toba Inlet area of British Columbia's Coast Mountains, was plucked from his campsite as he lay sleeping. The would-be miner reported that he was carried by a sasquatch to what seemed to be the beast's home. There were other such creatures at that encampment whom Ostman took to be his captor's immediate relatives.

Although he was not restrained in any way, the man stayed with the extraordinary family for six days. He reported that they were vegetarians and that their communication system was based on a series of sounds and signals.

In 1901, a sasquatch sighting near Campbell River on Vancouver Island was reported by several newspapers, including the *Victoria Colonist.* Mike King, a man described in the reports as "a fine type of man with an enviable reputation for reliability," had been scouting for timber stands to be logged. As he made his way throughout the Island's forested areas, guides who had been accompanying him suddenly refused to travel any further. They explained that the search was venturing dangerously close to lands where the dreaded "monkey-men" were thought to dwell.

With a confidence borne of naïvete, King made his way through the forest on his own until he came to a clearing surrounding a pool of water. What he saw at the edge of that pond must have instantly deflated King's ill-conceived cockiness. A large and powerful creature was crouched there, albeit placidly rinsing plant roots; King later described it as a "man-beast." He offered the following description of the animal's appearance—it is remarkably similar to other reports of the sasquatch: "Covered with reddish brown hair, and his arms were peculiarly long and were used freely in climbing and in brush running; whereas the trail showed a distinct human foot but with phenomenally long and spreading toes."

Slowly, it seemed, European explorers and settlers were learning that the tales of the huge hairy humanlike monster were not merely First Nations legends but factual reports, warnings to the wise. No longer did these newcomers wonder why so many sites around British Columbia's north-coastal town of Bella Coola carried names that included a word that the Europeans translated as "ape," for example, Ape Lake, Ape Creek, Ape Glacier and Ape Mountain. What had been initially thought to be the imaginings of the First Nations cultures were now being accepted as true accounts of dangerous creatures. Even as this realization was taking hold, occasional encounters with the sasquatch continued.

During the summer of 1906, a prospector told the newspaper *Yukon World* that he had recently seen a "wild man on the shores of Horn[e] Lake, [northeast of Port] Alberni." The man, who requested anonymity because he was "not looking for notoriety," described the beast as being "covered with a growth of hair much like ... bears," and added that it "ran with astonishing agility as soon as he saw us." He concluded his report by asserting, "That wild man is no figment of the imagination. You can take my word for that."

In October 1907, newspapers carried an article about a landowner near Vernon who found a giant footprint on one side of a 2-metre (6-foot) wide creek running through his property. There was an opposing print on the opposite bank. According to a report in the *Calgary Herald*, the impression was 48 centimetres (19 inches) in length, with the big toe alone measuring 13 centimetres (5 inches). People in the region flocked to see the strange prints. It was judged at the time that the creature whose foot left the mark would have had to have been at least 4 metres (13 feet) tall.

In October 1941, the *Edmonton Bulletin* newspaper carried banner headlines reading, "Beast Stands 10 Feet High, Paws 16 Inches Long, Trackers State." The incident being reported occurred roughly 170 kilometres (105 miles) east of the city of Vancouver. Reporter Alex Janusitis wrote, "Mrs. George Chapman of Ruby Creek reported that a 'hairy giant' ten feet [3 metres] tall and 'having the shape of a man covered with shaggy brown hair' had chased her and her four children from their home in the woods." (Other reports indicate that Mrs. Chapman had only two children: a boy, Jimmie, and a girl, Rosie.)

As this sighting of the strange creature was the third in two years, it caused quite a stir among Mrs. Chapman's neighbours. This latest encounter began when she heard her children, who had been playing in the backyard, suddenly scream.

"I looked out to see what had frightened the children and saw a huge hairy man about 10 feet [3 metres] tall coming from the direction of the barn. We fled to the woods and stayed there in the pouring rain for over three hours before we dared go back to the house," Mrs. Chapman explained.

Though the wet weather may not have been comfortable for the Chapmans hiding in the forest, it did serve to make the ground soft and therefore easily imprinted by the giant's feet. According to the article, "Mrs. Chapman said that the tracks left by the monster were 16" [41 centimetres] long, five inches [13 centimetres] across the heel and eight inches [20 centimetres] at the broad part of the foot."

The sighting caused some controversy between the two cultures in the immediate area. Those of European descent felt that the frightened family had misidentified a giant bear, whereas the Natives concurred that their heritage had long spoken of "a strange tribe of 'susquash' [*sic*] that inhabit the country ... and come out of their cave homes periodically to roam over a wide area, never stopping long at any one place."

With perhaps an air of smugness, or possibly optimism, the journalist writing about the Ruby Creek encounter concluded by stating, "Police and white settlers, however, have never taken the stories very seriously." Despite that generalization of the public's opinion, at least one family of "white settlers" apparently took the incident seriously—the Chapmans abandoned their cabin and moved on. That initiative was perhaps just as well because in May 1956 there was another sighting in the area. Stan Hunt, an auctioneer from Vernon, spotted two giant creatures on the opposite side of Ruby Creek.

A 1947 sighting was notable for three reasons: First, there were a pair of the animals, rather than just one. Second, they were quite close to civilization. Finally, the bodies of these two specimens were not covered just in their own hair. This unusual sasquatch observation was made by Nellie Werner and her husband while travelling up an old logging road on Grouse Mountain, only minutes from downtown Vancouver.

The creatures that the Werners saw were as large as those in other reports but they wore rudimentary clothing—their bodies were wrapped in cloaks of skins. Interestingly, as Mrs. Werner had at that time never heard of such a thing as a sasquatch, she simply presumed that they had happened upon "some sort of a wild man."

A statue of the sasquatch in Harrison Hot Springs—the next best thing to the real McCoy.

In 1957, a gentleman named William Roe swore out an affidavit attesting to an encounter that he'd had some two years earlier. He had been working with a highway crew near the east-central British Columbia town of Tête Jaune Cache, just west of Jasper, Alberta. During some time off he decided to explore the surroundings. While exploring, he saw off in the distance what he at first thought was a bear. As soon as the animal moved, Roe knew that he'd been wrong. That animal was no bear. The creature was just under 2 metres (6 feet) in height and 1 metre (3.3 feet) in breadth. It was covered from head to toe with silver-tipped dark brown hair.

Roe decided to hide from the strange creature and his tactic was effective, because he continued to have a clear view as it harvested and ate branches. He reported that he was close enough to accurately determine that this was a female of the species. He was also able to make out the facial features which, like other people who had encountered a sasquatch, he described as "flat."

Eventually the sasquatch detected Roe in the bushes and began to back away in fear. The man reported that, as he had a rifle with him, it had at first crossed his mind to shoot the animal and turn it over to scientists to examine. However, after having made eye-contact with it, Roe said that he could not bring himself to murder the thing.

In November 1962, Joe Gregg, a bus driver for Pacific Stage Lines, was returning from a late run to Canadian Forces Base Chilliwack when he spotted what he initially thought was a very large man wearing a fur coat standing at the side of the highway. Gregg slowed his vehicle and watched in amazement as the creature crossed the road in front of the bus. There was no question in the man's mind that he was observing a sasquatch. "He had enormous arms, enormous feet. He was at least seven feet [2.1 metres] tall and very agile."

Gregg was so distressed by what he'd witnessed that night that for five years he told no one, except his wife, about what he'd seen.

On June 28, 1965, two brothers were prospecting northeast of Vancouver in the Pitt Lake area. They came across "tremendous footprints" running through a valley and across a small, frozen stream. The weight of whatever had left the prints had cracked the ice and the prints picked up again on the opposite bank of the stream. The two were fascinated by their discovery and studied the imprints for some time. They estimated the length of a single print to be 60 centimetres (24 inches) and the width to be half that measurement.

The brothers followed the animal's trail until they came within sight of the creature. They knew instantly from other descriptions that they'd heard and read that they were gazing upon a sasquatch. They stopped and for some time watched the animal as it stood in one place, rocking back and forth. They had plenty of time to observe its features, which they later described as "flat."

Although the brothers would never allow themselves to be identified, they did agree to accompany a journalist with the *Vancouver Sun* in a helicopter as the reporter photographed the gargantuan footprints.

Even the decidedly non-sensationalist *Globe and Mail* carried a sasquatch-related report from Kaslo, a town on Kootenay Lake in the south of the province, during December 1978. Eighty-year-old Roy Green, a former mayor and councillor, had made a plaster cast of a 43-centimetre (17-inch) footprint that residents believed had been made by a sasquatch. He estimated that an animal with a footprint that large would have a stride 1.4 to 1.5 metres (4.5 to 5 feet) in length and weigh 270 to 360 kilograms (600 to 800 pounds).

Rex Alexander, a young man from the area, had found the prints while out hunting. Because of the secluded location in which he discovered the tracks, Alexander was convinced that they couldn't have been put there as a hoax.

"They were way off in the bush. It was just a fluke that I came across them."

Newspapers all over western Canada reported on a sasquatch sighting by Tim Meissener in April 1979. This sighting took place along the southern shore of Dunn Lake, just east of where Highway 24 joins Highway 1 north of Kamloops. Tim, who was sixteen at the time, immediately told his father, Ken, about spying a huge figure standing upright along the lakeshore. It had been about 100 metres (300 feet) from where he was, the young man explained. He had heard the creature utter a "high-pitched scream" before it fled, in an upright position, up a steep ravine.

When father and son returned to the spot later in the day, they found that a teepee-like structure had been constructed to cover a freshly killed deer. Further investigation revealed that the footprints of the animal that Tim had seen were shaped like a human's, but much larger—roughly 40 centimetres (16 inches) long. The distance between prints indicated that the creature had a stride nearly 2 metres (6 feet) long.

Though father and son were pleased with their unusual experience, the man who owned the land was not. Wayne Lahucik complained that, after the sasquatch sighting, his farm property was overrun with adventurers hoping for a glimpse at the unusual creature.

On November 11, 1989, many kilometres away from Dunn Lake, in the coastal town of Bella Coola, there was another sighting. This one also involved a sixteen-year-old youth, Jimmy Nelson, who was sitting with his mother and his friend, Glen Clellamin, at the family's kitchen table. First one and then another of the trio detected a terrible odour, an odour that hadn't been present just moments before.

Curious, Glen looked out the kitchen window and saw what he at first thought was a bear. He called the others to the window and together they watched as the bad-smelling animal, which was definitely not a bear, fled, on two feet, into the woods. They all agreed that the creature that they'd seen was almost 3 metres (10 feet) in height, had enormous shoulders, and ran as a human being would.

With the courage of youth, the two boys pursued the strange creature. They were less than 10 metres (30 feet) from it when it turned, glared at them and growled. The boys may have been young and brave, but they were not foolish. They turned tail and ran back to the Nelsons' cabin. The next day they headed out again to investigate further. This time there was no sign of the animal itself, just the tracks that its feet had made as it fled.

The foregoing accounts describe some of the sasquatch sightings that have taken place over the years in British Columbia. Many additional encounters have been reported and, no doubt, very many more than that have *not* been reported.

Ogopogo and Other "Water Monsters"

A palindrome is a word or phrase that reads the same backward or forward. Such word games are at best fun and challenging. At worst, they're uninteresting and frustrating. It's difficult, though, to imagine being afraid of a palindrome—unless it happens to be the name of Canada's best-known water monster, Ogopogo, and you suddenly find yourself face to face with it!

Imagine that it's the summer of 1977 and you are a youngster, part of a group, enjoying a perfect summer day at extraordinarily beautiful Okanagan Lake. Someone suggests water-skiing. You don't even think of saying "no." You wait patiently until it's your turn to don the skis. Despite your best efforts to brace them, your legs quake a bit as the tow-rope between you and the boat tightens. The shakiness comes partly from excitement and anticipation of the adventure ahead, partly from the momentary challenge of standing up.

Then you're upright and enjoying the strange sense of freedom that comes with water-skiing. It's strange because you're most assuredly not free at all: you are tethered to a powerful boat. However, if it were not for that tether (and the physics entailed in how it affects your motion), you would not be enjoying that exhilarating—if deceptive—feeling of freedom.

Once you have the feel of the skis, the water, the rope, the boat and its operator's style, that bit of tension that you felt begins to melt away. You relax, cutting in and out of the wake. The stream lifts you up ever so briefly before your skis slap down hard on the water's surface. Any worries that you might have had before getting out there in the middle of Okanagan Lake are washed away by the drops of water being sprayed against your body.

Suddenly your eyes fall on something in the water—something that isn't supposed to really exist. There, not 1 metre (3 feet) from you, is a huge, ugly creature, staring directly into your eyes. Your concentration instantly shattered, you drop the line that would have pulled you away from the frightful beast. You land in the water, in the middle of a lake that some people say is bottomless, right beside what you'd always thought was a mythical water monster. Your subconscious reflexes intended to preserve your well-being kick in and you faint. But, because you're in the water, the faint becomes life-threatening rather than life-preserving.

The story above may sound like an imaginative anecdote, but it recounts exactly what happened to Erin Neely on July 2, 1977. Fortunately, the tale has a happy ending. The ski-boat's operator manoeuvred his craft skilfully and quickly enough to save Erin's young life. According to an article in a November 1978 edition of *The Smithsonian* magazine, the terrifying incident put Erin in the unusual, but perhaps not enviable, position of being only one of two people to have experienced Ogopogo "up close and personal" and lived to tell of it.

Non-Native exposure to the monster said to inhabit Okanagan Lake began in the late 1850s, when pioneers began settling in south-central British Columbia. The First Nations people made it a point to warn the newcomers of the grave danger lurking in the deep waters of the long, narrow lake that would come to be known as Okanagan Lake. No Native would be foolish enough to attempt to cross the lake without loading at least one small animal, often a pig or a dog, into his canoe. That way, at the first sign of the dreaded monster's approach—usually indicated by turbulence in the water—he could throw the animal overboard as a sacrifice to temporarily appease the monster of the lake, *Nha-a-tik.* (I have chosen to use the Salish spelling because it is one of the most common one of the eight or more that exist.)

Initially the settlers around the lake scoffed at the tales of the First Nations peoples. They found such stories to be whimsical and inventive—certainly not anything to be taken seriously. It wasn't until the mid-1860s that the potential danger involved in crossing the lake became apparent to the burgeoning community of pioneers.

John MacDougall, a man whose parents represented both the aboriginal and immigrant communities, gambled with the myth and lost. He set out to lead his horses across the Narrows. Paddling a canoe, MacDougall started his horses swimming. For unrecorded reasons, he did not bring the standard precautionary sacrifice. Well before he made it to the safety of the opposite shore, an unseen force pulled MacDougall's animals under. They were never seen again.

By the mid-1870s, immigrants were paying considerably more attention to the First Nations perspective. Two of the most respected settlers, Susan Allison and Thomas Smitheram, had actually seen the monster. The two were not together at the time, and yet their sightings were made on the same day, but from opposite shores of the lake. Their descriptions of the monster were identical.

Mrs. Allison, who was well aware of the legend about the lake monster, was watching for her husband and son to return from a nearby mission. She stood at the edge of a bluff on her family's ranch property overlooking Westbank (across the lake from Kelowna). The storm that had swept through the area over the previous night had abated—all but the strong northerly winds that continued to blow along the length of the lake.

At some point, what appeared to be a large log on the lake caught her eye. Her initial reaction may have been some concern for the potential danger that the log might present to anyone on the lake in a small craft. If so, that concern was no doubt increased when she saw the huge "log" begin to move, to swim against the current whipped up by the winds.

When Susan Allison saw that movement, her sceptical attitude toward the tales of *Nha-a-tik,* the water monster, were no doubt altered forever. She realized that what she'd seen was indeed a giant reptile and, from that day on, the story of the monster in the lake was accepted as a cross-cultural one.

Roughly twenty-five years later, a ten-year-old girl playing on a beach at Okanagan Landing, near Vernon, unwittingly entered into a short, but intense, visual exchange with the monster. The child, Ruth Richardson, saw the creature staring at her. Then she watched as it submerged—only to reappear seconds later, much closer to the spot where she knelt, momentarily transfixed in her terror. Ruth fled as soon as she could force her legs to obey the orders issued by her brain.

The encounter so terrified Ruth Richardson that when, as an adult, she returned to the spot where she'd seen the water monster, she reportedly turned down all invitations to go out on the lake in a boat. Richardson was quoted at that time as saying that she would not venture out onto those waters "for any money." There was clearly no doubt in the woman's mind that the stories of the huge beast beneath the waves of Okanagan Lake were all too real.

And so, the settlers' awareness of the existence of the potentially dangerous beast began to increase. Sailors aboard vessels that plied the lake's waters often reported catching glimpses of the mysterious being. The authorities formed hunting parties to rid the lake of the creature whose existence they had once disbelieved.

Interestingly, some twenty years after those (unsuccessful) assassination plots were being developed, the "enemy" was given the cute name of "Ogopogo," which is still in use. The appellation is believed to have originated in a parody of the words in an old English music-hall tune. The revised rhyme indicated that "his mother was an earwig; his father was a whale." Since the creature's appearance so defied any plausible attempt at identifying its true ancestry, the mention of earwigs and whales succeeded in bringing the animal into a more familiar realm.

Ogopogo has gone from being treated as a dreaded beast that has to be appeased by live offerings of small sacrificial animals to being depicted as an appealing, and even lovable, cartoon-character sort of monster. If it exists—and there have been enough sightings to suggest that it does—Ogopogo is probably neither. Most often witnesses describe seeing a snakelike creature anywhere from 3.5 to 21 metres (11 to 70 feet) in length. It is usually described as having humps and being either black or very dark green. We do know that it travels very quickly in the water, but there is uncertainty as to how it propels itself. Its head is sometimes said to resemble a goat's and, at other times, a dog's or, more fittingly, given the descriptions of its body, a snake's.

So, if our opinions have changed that drastically, does that mean that we've learned more about the beast, which is reputed to live in an underwater cave near Squally Point in Okanagan Lake? Unfortunately, not significantly. Theories explaining (or refuting) the existence of the creature are as controversial now as they ever were.

There have been enough reports from reliable witnesses over the years to conclude that there is at least one unusual large creature in Okanagan Lake. And, although Ogopogo is usually each referred to as a singular entity, it is highly unlikely that there ever was only one such creature. Reliable witnesses have reported seeing more than one of the strange creatures at the same time in the lake.

Ogopogo is no longer suspected of being some kind of a freshwater manatee because it is too big and moves too quickly to be a member of that group. One school of thought maintains that people think that they see one animal, but that they are actually observing a number of large sturgeon swimming in a line. Proponents of that theory like to remind people that sturgeon in British Columbia have apparently reached lengths of 4 metres (13 feet) and weights of 400 kilograms (880 pounds).

Is Ogopogo a throw-back, a prehistoric land animal that, in order to preserve itself, adapted to living in the water? Evidence, in the form of enormous footprints on land, has been found to support that theory. Descriptions of both Ogopogo and its supposed cousin, Nessie, the monster in Scotland's Loch Ness, suggest a resemblance to the long-extinct plesiosaurs. Or they may be sea serpents that have become landlocked and are able to survive, and even thrive, on the plentiful supply of food in the lake and that they mostly escape detection by hiding in submerged crevices and caves. Given that Ogopogo's home, Okanagan Lake, is 170 kilometres (105 miles) long and over 300 metres (980 feet) deep in places, there is certainly plenty of space for any or all of these theories to take hold and grow.

All these theories have both their supporters and their detractors. The giant sturgeon hypothesis can be quickly deflated with the knowledge that sturgeon are bottom feeders who rarely come up from the depths. The assumption that the animal does not really exist, but is the result of either creative imaginations or optical illusions, is defeated by the photographs that exist of the beast.

Most scientists are sceptical nonetheless. However, in his paper *The Population Density of Monsters in Loch Ness*, British Columbia's

Dr. Stephen Kerr maintained that, "At a time when physicists work with quarks and black holes and attribute properties such as charm and strangeness to subatomic particles I would not be surprised at anything."

Maybe not, but on July 29, 1962, the thirty people attending a church picnic were certainly surprised to see an enormous, snake-like creature that moved through the water "like a caterpillar." And what of the rotting carcass found back in 1914 on Rattlesnake Island? The island lies near Squally Point where, it is generally believed, Ogopogo's underwater cave is located. The find gave people their first opportunity to view and examine the monster in detail and safety.

F.R. Buckland, a member of the party that made the find, described the gargantuan body as being blue-gray in colour, sparsely covered with hair, having a flat tail, no visible neck or ears and a stubby nose protruding from a rounded head. The animal's appendages were flippers equipped with claws.

Portions of the enormous skeleton found that day were displayed to the public. Not surprisingly, the exhibition drew interested folks from all over. After all, it's not every day that a person has the opportunity to gaze upon shoulder bones 2 metres (6.5 feet) in breadth, along with tusks and claws, that were taken from a corpse that was estimated to weigh in excess of 180 kilograms (400 pounds).

To "muddy the waters" of investigation even further, it must be recognized that Ogopogo is not the only water monster in Canada. Far from it. These creatures—unidentified swimming objects (USOs), as they are sometimes called—can be found in other provinces as well. A heritage painting held by the New Brunswick Museum shows two people in a canoe as they try desperately to paddle away from an enormous snakelike creature that is pursuing them. A monster sometimes referred to as "Manipogo," and at other times as "Winnipogo," is thought to dwell in the depths of Manitoba's Lake Winnipeg. In the 1800s there were reports of a monster in Quebec's Lake Pohenegamook. The Turtle Lake Monster in Saskatchewan has, for years, been held responsible for shredding fishing nets. In Ontario, Kempenfelt Kelly makes its home under the surface of Lake Simcoe.

We have other, less well-known, mysterious water-dwelling beasts right here in British Columbia. Human knowledge of these creatures dates back to long before non-Natives began to explore the area. The beasts have been reported in the lore of the First Nations peoples for centuries. Depictions of dragonlike sea serpents appear among the rock etchings at Petroglyph Park just south of Nanaimo. In 1881, Frank Stannard, then a boy of twelve, armed with a slingshot and a supply of small stones, struck just such a monster near there.

In 1903, a sighting near the Bamfield cable station on the west coast of Vancouver Island at Barkley Sound made national headlines. The article describes the April 14 sighting of "a sea serpent from forty to sixty feet [12 to 18 metres] long with a head like a horse." Although doubtless startled, the witnesses could not have been entirely surprised by the sighting, for the First Nations people in the area "had been telling [them] of the existence of a sea serpent." The report adds that, with the typical arrogance of settlers, those warnings were disregarded. On this spring day, however, technically trained men watched the strange creature "raise a big horse-like head and swim out from the mouth of Bamfield Creek into Barclay [*sic*] Sound." The witnesses must have been impressed by the speed of the animal's movement, for they reported that "it moved off with the speed of a torpedo boat."

When word of the sighting spread to the community outside the station, the operators learned that, just four days previously, local Natives had made similar observations.

Other monsters have been reported in the waters around Vancouver Island over the last 150 years. During April 1929, in Haro Strait near D'Arcy Island off Central Saanich, two fishermen reported seeing a sea serpent. On the other side of the Saanich Peninsula, and just over a decade later, two of the people stationed at Patricia Bay, Leading Aircraftsman C.O. Biscaro and Aircraftsman W.F. Hinde, will likely never forgot that particular posting. In July of 1940, while on the water in a small craft, the two men came far too close for comfort to a creature "with fins all over its looped body."

Nine years later, a pair of water monsters were observed in Swartz Bay, at the northeastern tip of the peninsula. As recently as 1963, Mr. and Mrs. Dave Welham of Saltair (about halfway between Duncan and Nanaimo) watched what looked like a giant eel playing in a cove off Stuart Channel. Over the years there have been sea-serpent sightings made from numerous places around Vancouver Island, including Qualicum Beach, Chemainus, Campbell River and other locations.

These various creatures are often referred to simply as "Caddy" because the huge beast has often been seen in Cadboro Bay near the University of Victoria campus. Aside from Ogopogo, Caddy is probably the best known of Canada's USOs. Like Ogopogo, Caddy had a long and rich heritage before settlers arrived in the area. Since then he has managed to capture the attentions of those relative newcomers.

Encounters with Caddy or his cousins were especially frequent in the 1930s. In 1932, Hubert Evans, at the time a well-respected resident of Roberts Creek (on the Sunshine Coast), and his friend Dick Reeve were looking out over the water toward Vancouver

Island. Some fifty years after the fact he described the sighting succinctly and colourfully as "the damndest [*sic*] thing."

The water in Georgia Strait had been as calm as glass, he recalled. Seconds later, the water's surface was broken by a "series of bumps" after which a "shaft" 2 to 3 metres (6 to 10 feet) tall protruded just ahead of the bumps. The shaft then turned so that Evans and Reeve were able to see that it was in actuality a neck with a head at the end. The man recalled that the head, which had clearly defined facial features, was roughly equivalent in size and shape to a horse's. Evans acknowledged that the sighting unnerved the two men, declaring, "It just put the hair up on the back of your neck."

Once they had composed themselves sufficiently, the men looked for a camera. They found one, but there was no film at hand. Though Evans and his companion weren't able to photograph the animal, he did note that someone else must also have seen the strange beast, because the police had been notified and had sent a boat out to observe and record details about the thing.

For some time from that day onward, the monster was seen often. Some witnesses were more credible than others and some cases have, therefore, become better known than others.

An example of an instance that was taken very seriously occurred on October 8, 1933. Major W.H. Langley, a local lawyer who held the position of Clerk of the Legislature, and his wife were out in Cadboro Bay on their sailboat early one Sunday afternoon. Major Langley was an experienced sailor who was familiar with marine life after spending many years on whaling ships and yet, even at close range, he was not able to identify the species of the strange creature in front of them. He did note that it was nearly 30 metres (100 feet) in length "and as wide as an average automobile."

Langley reported the experience to the press who, of course, ran an article about this high-profile and respected citizen spotting the much-talked-about sea monster. The article prompted a reply from a government employee attesting that he too had recently seen the beast, but had chosen to keep mum in order to avoid public ridicule.

Ever since that minor flurry of excitement, the sea monster associated with Cadboro Bay has been affectionately known as "Caddy."

On December 6, 1938, the tugboat *Catala Chief* was in Stuart Channel, roughly 30 kilometres (20 miles) south of Nanaimo, when the captain and crew spotted a serpent "looping through the waters" that fit the general description of Caddy. The first creature was then joined by a second, similar one.

The following year, four young men were heading to Vancouver in a fishing boat when they spotted Caddy. "I could clearly see the monster," Victor Johnson, one of the men, told a reporter. Just two weeks later, on March 15, 1939, the *Vancouver Sun* playfully referred to the monster as "Mr. Cadborosaurus" after it had been spotted off Chemainus.

The waters near Victoria are believed by many people to be home to an unidentified swimming object.

Then, early in January 1940, Cecil Burgess and Norman Ingram, two Victoria residents, reported being "glared at" from a distance of some 12 metres (40 feet) by eyes set in a head that "resembled a cross between that of a camel and a walrus." The body of the animal that they saw was, like in the Johnson sighting, nearly 1 metre (3 feet) thick. Neither of the two men or any of the several other witnesses offered an estimate of the animal's overall length.

During the last half of April 1950, several residents of Sidney (north of Victoria), including two women whose names were recorded as "Mrs. Dan Butler" and "Mrs. H. Bradley," reported seeing a serpentlike creature about 35 metres (115 feet) out from the shore. They estimated the animal as being nearly 20 metres (65 feet) in length, having a "long, slender neck" that was apparently dark brown and just less than 0.5 metres (1.5 feet) in diameter. This neck held up a head that the women described as "peculiar" and "pointed."

Sightings continued, and continue to the present day, with the summer of 1997 having been especially busy with Caddy sightings. Local newspapers carried reports of credible sightings. In one article, retired cryptozoologist (someone who studies "hidden" animals) Dr. Ed Bousfield explained Cadborosaurus as a "Mesozoic relic."

In reference to a sighting by two University of Victoria students the following month, Dr. Bousfield stated that the reptilelike Caddy is "probably one of the last living dinosaurs." His research over the years had indicated that—rather than lay eggs, as one would expect of a reptile—"the females come to shores of shallow estuaries to bear live young."

A few pictures exist of the beast but, during the summer of 1951, an American tourist who tried to take Caddy's photograph managed only to get his own version of the classic "big one that got away" story.

It seems that Don McIntyre was visiting Victoria from his home in Los Angeles. On Saturday, July 25, he rented a boat and headed out to enjoy some time on the waters of Brentwood Bay. As luck would have it, Caddy made one of its unpredictable appearances and McIntyre was ready with his waterproof camera. The animal raised its head and the photographer snapped a shot. Unfortunately he became nervous and his camera slipped from his grasp—and fell into the depths below.

In keeping with the tradition of such sad tales, Don McIntyre assured a reporter for the *Vancouver Sun* that the photograph that he took would have been "a beauty."

The monster sighted in Thetis Lake, north of Victoria, during a three-day period in August of 1972, however, was anything but a beauty. From drawings that the frightened witnesses created after their encounter, it closely resembled the monster in the movie *Creature from the Black Lagoon.* The strange "gill-man" reported to have emerged from the waters of Thetis Lake was apparently a bipedal reptile with six spikes atop its head. It was also aggressive. As the creature emerged from the water, it spotted the small group of people standing nearby on the shore. Terrified, the people ran. The beast chased after them and is reported to have gotten close enough to cut one man's hand with one of its head spikes.

In total, water monsters have been reported in at least two dozen British Columbia lakes. Cryptozoologists believe that, with a few exceptions, the creatures in these lakes and in coastal waters generally have one of two different appearances. According to local expert Jim Clark, one type, like Ogopogo, has a long neck and a doglike face. The other type resembles a giant squid but has a seaweed-coloured mane.

All of these strange beasts—land dwellers such as the sasquatch and water dwellers such as Ogopogo and Caddy—have terrified and fascinated humans for centuries. And yet, interest in the creatures is not waning. Far from it. If anything, investigative approaches have become more serious and intensive.

Surprising as it may seem, these creatures are protected by law: It is illegal to harm any one of them. By inference, this protection supports the claim that such hidden oddities do actually exist.

At this writing, John Kirk, a British Columbia-based expert on the Okanagan Lake's monster, is preparing for a thorough on-site exploration of the creature's habitat in the year 2000. He feels some urgency is involved, as he fears that the species may be in danger of becoming extinct.

It will be interesting to note any progress that might be made toward overcoming centuries of fear. Considering that in 1938 a South African fishing trawler hauled up the carcass of a coelacanth, a fish that scientists were sure had been extinct for sixty million years, there is reason to believe that we will eventually know the explanation for these supernatural British Columbia enigmas of the aquatic variety. But what about unidentified flying objects, which have been seen over the province since the nineteenth century—and possibly much earlier?

Unidentified Flying Objects

Note that the phrase "unidentified flying object" (UFO), as it is used in this book, is intended to mean just that—a flying object of unknown identity, not necessarily a spaceship from another planet.

At different times in its history, the sky over British Columbia has been a veritable hotbed of UFO activities and sightings, with some encounters even predating non-Native settlement. In the late 1700s, when Captain John Meares was exploring the Nootka Sound area on the west coast of Vancouver Island, First Nations people told him of extraordinary visitors arriving from the skies in "metallic canoes." Since that time, and up to the present day, we can find references to UFOs being seen in the airspace above supernatural British Columbia.

To examine the phenomenon in this area, it is necessary that we begin with a brief overview of what was, without doubt, the most dramatic single UFO incident in recent times: the purported crash landing of an occupied spacecraft near Roswell, New Mexico.

It is widely believed, and just as widely denied, that on July 2, 1947, an alien spaceship plummeted to Earth there, eventually killing all of those on board. The next morning, rancher Mac Brazel, who owned the land on which the accident occurred, found debris strewn about his property. Not only could he not account for the detritus, he could not even identify it. Baffled, he called in the authorities and the controversy over what was found, what caused the debris and what its origins were, remains unsettled to this day.

Many fascinating books have been written about Roswell and, as a result, the incident is more widely known today than it was immediately after the supposed crash occurred. Interest in the case has become so pervasive that on July 2, 1997, fifty years after the incident, hundreds of people flocked to the small New Mexico community to acknowledge what they felt was one of the world's most significant events.

What is less well known, however, is that fifty years *before* the events at Roswell, UFO sightings were making worldwide headlines on an almost daily basis, especially right here in British Columbia. However, a factor in the number of sightings during the summer of 1897 was that many people were watching the sky in hopes of seeing even a remnant of what had become known as "Andree's balloon."

"Andree" was Scandinavian inventor Dr. Salomon August Andree. He and three companions had set out from Norway on July 11, 1897, in an attempt to cross the North Pole in a balloon. People were intrigued by his planned escapade and looked forward to learning about his adventures. Unfortunately, although Andree claimed to be well equipped for a safe voyage, he, his crew and their balloon disappeared not long after take-off. It was not until 1930 that the craft's ruins were found. They were on White Island, not far from Spitsbergen, Norway. According to researcher W. Ritchie Benedict of Calgary, Alberta, it is widely presumed that "their balloon trip had lasted all of three days."

The fact that the balloon had not gotten far did not prevent worldwide reports of "Andree sightings" throughout most of the summer of 1897. These reports were given a great deal of attention by the press and references to Andree and his balloon were often included in the many UFO reports from British Columbia residents during that summer.

Reports in local papers of a wave of UFO sightings, and their resulting furore, began in July 1897. Headlines in the Victoria *Daily Colonist* proclaimed news of "That Pillar of Fire." Below the headline were three subheads: "The Mysterious Visitor Seen Again Drifting over Northern British Columbia," "Rivers Inlet Fishermen Watch for Two Hours the Powerful Moving Light" and "Visible by Daylight as Well as before Dawn and Mistaken for Andree's Balloon."

Vancouver Island fisherman W. S. Fitzgerald wrote a letter to the *Daily Colonist* describing what had happened one night while they were "drifting for salmon out at the mouth of Rivers Inlet." A light "soaring smoothly along in boundless space" almost 2 kilometres (1.2 miles) above the highest mountain peak in their horizon caught their attention.

"It couldn't be a fire[,] we knew, nor a star, nor yet the moon. The night was dark and overcast and when it first came into view it was through a rift in a black mass of clouds. There seemed to be besides the powerful light a large pear-shaped body attached and rendered luminous by the reflection of that light. We saw it pass through rift after rift of clouds. It was evidently moving in a different atmosphere or currents of air, than [those that] we felt below at the time, for whereas on the water there was a nasty squally wind blowing, it seemed to glide majestically along without so much as a tremor," Fitgerald explained.

Fascinated by what they were seeing, the pair watched the UFO until the light of morning made it harder to see and the object finally "disappeared behind a huge mass of dark clouds."

This public report brought forth information that, some days earlier, two employees of Victoria's Electric Light Company had seen "a balloon-shaped light rising slowly in the eastern sky." Soon afterward, people near Kamloops described seeing a similar object.

Reports of sightings continued into August. One undoubtedly long-deceased scribe referred to "that strange aerial curiosity" and went on to speculate as to where the "fire balloon" might have come from or where it went during those times when it was not visible over British Columbia. He also acknowledged that two Victoria firefighters, North and Swain by name, watched the craft "floating low" over the horizon while it was "mirrored in the waters of the Straits [and] hanging over Discovery Island [east of Victoria]."

This report, however, added another dimension to the mystery in that witnesses attested that the object "had no discernible form" but rather "was just a great light ... [like] ... the sun at high noon." The activities of this light held the two men fascinated for more than two hours. They watched as "it slowly rose and then took a westerly direction." Realizing that they were observing the craft that had been causing such a stir, the men left their posts to get a third man, a night clerk at a nearby hotel, to share in and to attest to their encounter.

Later in August, E. Scrope Shrapnel of Oak Bay declared that he and members of his family had "watched the same brilliant light swaying from side to side slowly, and sometimes rising and falling."

Is that a UFO in the sky over Georgia Strait? A ghost light?

He declared with certainty "It was decidedly no reflection," but "brighter than the numerous stars in view."

By now, virtually the entire British Columbia population was abuzz with the sightings. The unidentified flying object was still seen from Vancouver Island, but now also from the Lower Mainland, as well as from south-central British Columbia. Witnesses numbered in the thousands and interest was growing on a daily basis. Surprisingly, judging from the tone of newspaper reports that summer, people were more fascinated with than fearful of whatever it was that they were seeing. One scribe demonstrated the predominant attitude clearly when he ended his report with the following sentence: "After showing its respects to Rossland, the wonder made several wide circles, like a bird undecided [as to] what course to pursue, and then struck an air line [set a course] and passed rapidly away towards the south."

By mid-August 1897, many of the words used to describe the "fiery vision" were similar to those that witnesses still use today. The words "mystery" or "mysterious" were more common than "unidentified," but descriptions of the objects' shapes began to include phrases such as "cigar-shaped" and "a globe."

A comparison of write-ups from Vancouver and Rossland, hundreds of kilometres to the east, indicates that people in both centres were in all likelihood looking at the same object.

The journalist from Rossland chose especially evocative phrases: "When first observed it was hull down on the horizon, but [it] approached with the swiftness of light, and after hovering about for over a quarter of an hour poised in mid air, surrounding itself the while with flashes of colors, it streaked off in a southerly direction and soon faded from sight. Little particles of fire seemed to shoot out from the main ball and then a flash of red followed. It looked for all the world like a lighthouse with a revolving flashlight of colors."

By autumn of 1897, no new reports appeared in the British Columbia papers. The public's fascination with the celestial display that they'd been treated to over the summer months continued, however, as witnessed by the rehashing of previous reports. An October 7, 1897, headline noted that "A Learned Publication Deals With the Aerial Mystery." That review of the summer's strange activities, which referred to *The Canadian Engineer*, was carried in the Victoria *Daily Colonist* and advised the newspaper's readers that the mysterious display of lights had been seen in the skies over many parts of Canada.

The wave of excitement was apparently over by the end of 1897 and it was fully another fifty years before a suspected alien spacecraft would again cause such a significant stir. The lack of public focus did not mean that sightings of UFOs over British Columbia had ceased—new reports were registered in every subsequent decade.

During August 1924, newspapers all over western Canada carried a report about the "mysterious signals picked up at Point Grey wireless station" in Vancouver. Scientists listening to the sounds wondered whether possibly some intelligent lifeform on Mars was "trying to establish communication with Earth." They were not able to discern what the pattern of signals might have meant, but they were convinced that the disturbance was meaningful.

In the words of radio operator W.T. Burford, "The fact that I distinctly got four groups of four dashes convinced me that some intelligible communication force was at work." If the nature of that force was ever uncovered, the discovery was not reported in the newspapers.

Although sightings of UFOs over British Columbia continued throughout the next dozen years, official reports of such events tended to be relegated to the back pages of newspapers. Understandably, news of the Great Depression and the Second World War were of utmost concern to citizens during that time. In mid-1947, however, there was a resurgence of UFO visitations, or least of their reporting. Whatever the cause, the "modern era" of unidentified flying objects had begun and people were in for a summer of UFOs such as had not been seen since the rash of sightings fifty years before in 1897.

On June 24, 1947, private pilot Kenneth Arnold was flying in the area over Yakima, Washington. He was travelling at an altitude of just over 3 kilometres (2 miles) when a fleet of "nine crescent-shaped objects" came into view. He described them as "flat, [and] disclike, like pie tins, with highly polished surfaces, moving at a high rate of speed." Arnold noted that the UFOs' actions were not aggressive toward him.

Kenneth Arnold reported his observations and people were fascinated. The United States Air Force, however, announced that the man had merely seen "a mirage." Just days before the mysterious crash at Roswell was to occur, there was already an obvious discrepancy between reports from the public and the official position, leading to ongoing opportunities for speculation by conspiracy theorists.

Given their proximity to the State of Washington, it is not surprising that the citizens of British Columbia were also in on the leading edge of the UFO debate. On June 27, 1947, Victoria resident William Crodie told reporters that, in the early evening, he'd been "mystified" by a "silvery object without wings or tail" flying in the sky toward the horizon.

"It was sinking slowly, so I couldn't tell whether it was going straight away from me or dropping," Crodie explained.

Unintentionally foreshadowing the fallout from the watershed event that was to occur just five days later in Roswell, "a U.S. Army rocket expert" from New Mexico, Lieutenant Colonel Harold

R. Turner, stated emphatically that the object of Crodie's sighting was simply a misidentified "jet plane." The article in the *Sun* concluded with the words of witness Mrs. E.G. Peterson, who clearly disagreed with the official stance. She told a journalist that what she'd seen, "didn't look like jet ships or anything else" that she'd ever seen before.

Today, more than one hundred years after the host of dramatic UFO sightings that captivated the imaginations of many North Americans, and more than fifty years after the sightings in British Columbia that anticipated the news from Roswell, reviewing the articles about the various sightings over the years has been a provocative activity. During my research I became intrigued by the similarity between some accounts of UFOs and some descriptions of ignes fatui (ghost lights). Of the many UFO reports available, I have selected for inclusion in this book mainly the ones that resemble the ghost light accounts, though I have also included a few others that I found especially compelling.

In August 1948, farmers near Duncan on Vancouver Island reported watching "a centre of light overhead." They had no idea what it was that they were observing, but did note that their cattle reacted to its presence by "charging around."

In northern British Columbia, witnesses stared in wonder when, on St. Patrick's Day (March 17), 1950, they observed an object that they labelled a "flying saucer." Their descriptions of the mysterious craft in the sky included terms similar to both those used back in 1897 and in the 1947 Roswell incident. They spoke of "a strange cylindrical translucent object" soaring roughly 200 metres (650 feet) over the harbour. "It appeared to be of some sort of fabric of a silvery translucent nature" according to Hubert Ward, a marine surveyor. The strange object flew northward out of view at an altitude of approximately 1 kilometre (3300 feet).

A few days later, at Trail, not far from the Rossland sighting of 1897, an encounter with a UFO was once again dealt with by the press in a decidedly lighthearted vein. The reporter opened a story about Mrs. J.E. Doyle's having watched a UFO with a reference to "little men from another planet" taking" a gander" at south-central British Columbia. Mrs. Doyle declared that whatever it was that she'd seen "was no ordinary aircraft" and that it was travelling "awfully fast" as it disappeared beyond the mountains.

Another cluster of British Columbia-based UFO sightings was recorded during the last three months of 1959. In the Okanagan Valley of south-central British Columbia, residents both heard and saw a light-coloured circular object moving from east to west across the sky above their homes. Just west of the town of Oliver, the airborne body turned in a southerly direction. It then hovered there before suddenly picking up speed and disappearing from sight.

Dick Lloyd, one of the people reporting the event, watched the craft through binoculars. He later described it as looking "like two shallow soup bowls face to face with a distinct edge or lip." He added that the object was definitely flying and looked to be pulsating. Reports from other residents of the area echoed Lloyd's descriptions. In addition, the citizens of Duncan on Vancouver Island had reported similar sightings just a few days earlier.

The first years of the 1960s were remarkably quiet. If UFOs were seen over British Columbia, those observations were apparently not reported to, or by, the media. By 1969, however, write-ups about

UFOs—and even photographs of them—had once again begun to dot British Columbia's newspapers.

In mid-October 1974, eleven-year-old David Knutsen noticed two RCMP officers in a parking lot near his home in Surrey. They were standing still, staring and pointing toward the sky above them. When David followed their line of vision, he was most surprised to see a dark-coloured disk approximately 135 metres (450 feet) away. He ran for his camera and was able to photograph the disk before it "took off super fast."

George Thrupp and Margaret Mancor were driving through a section of the Vancouver International Airport in April 1977 when a blue flash in the sky caught their eye. They described how they had stared in awe at an orange-and-blue cigar-shaped object. It was bigger than a jumbo jet, they explained, and had portholes along its side. Seconds later, the soundless object had disappeared.

Some twenty-one years after that sighting, an even more dramatic one reportedly occurred near the same airport. A British magazine specializing in UFO sightings received a letter from a man living in nearby Delta. The body of the letter detailed an account of a startling incident.

Just after six o'clock in the evening of May 26, 1998, a 767 jet owned by a courier company was over Vancouver Island to the southwest of Vancouver International Airport. The pilot radioed the traffic controllers to ask if they had knowledge of any other planes in his immediate vicinity. The controller who took the man's question replied in the negative, for no other planes were nearby at that moment. The courier pilot continued on his route but, as he did, he informed the people in the tower that he found their response odd, since he had just witnessed a "shiny, metallic object" resembling a missile flying under his plane as it headed in the opposite direction.

Understandably, the controller asked the pilot to repeat his communication. Despite the pilot's reiteration of the event, the controller could offer no explanation for the object's dangerous proximity to the jet.

Less than six months later, on November 9, just before 7:30 in the morning, a plane flying over the Queen Charlotte Islands contacted the nearest air traffic control station to ask if there were any planes to be aware of in the area. The controller indicated that no other aircraft was within 370 kilometres (200 nautical miles) of their location. Although this information would normally have been good news, on this occasion the report of vacant skies did nothing to console the pilot, for he had just seen first three orange objects and then two white ones.

Grasping for an explanation, the staff in the control tower suggested, perhaps hopefully, that what the pilot had seen were meteors. The man in the cockpit, an experienced flyer, replied simply, "They're not meteors."

One of the most dramatic sightings in Canada came from a child in Westbank, very near the presumed home of Ogopogo. Although Dawn Smith was only nine years old in 1978 when this encounter occurred, UFO experts who've heard her story were impressed with its authenticity.

On a November morning, a bright object in the sky caught the child's attention. Scrambling to her bedroom window for a better look, she watched in fascination as two bright lights, a large green one and a small white one, bobbed up and down in the still-dark sky.

She realized that the lights were attached to two craft of some kind and noted that there were actually several green lights, not just one. Moments later, the smaller of the two craft disappeared inside the larger one. Red lights then became visible along with the green ones and, moments later, the craft disappeared from view.

Now that you have read a few accounts of the many UFO sightings that have been made in the skies above British Columbia, I repeat the caution that I use the term "UFO" to truly mean "*unidentified* flying object" and not necessarily an alien spacecraft. I can only wonder—do the mystery lights that some people see originate from the hulls of interstellar ships or are they ghost lights? In cases like the one described in "A Bizarre Old Story" (p. 153), where the tale may have lost some details over time, it can be hard to be sure without additional evidence. The paranormal world, especially that of supernatural British Columbia, seems to defy ready understanding.

As acknowledged in the introduction to this book, if "the truth is out there," it has certainly eluded me in my investigations so far. If you have any information that you believe might help to solve any of the wonderful mysteries referred to in this book, I would love to hear from you.

All across the length and breadth of Canada are multitudes of spine-tingling ghost stories that will have you checking under your bed, behind your closet door and in your basement. The tales involve almost any place in the country, from houses and historic sites, to trains, churches, schools, hospitals and theatres. Stories range from long-dead relatives returning for a last look at a loved one, to mysterious flashing lights and crashing noises, apparitions dating back hundreds of years, unresolved murders, curses, ghost ships, phantom beasts, buried treasure and more.